SIT
STILL
AND
Listen

SIT
STILL
AND
Listen

Lyn Partridge-Webber. Wellington Witch

authorHOUSE®

AuthorHouse™ UK Ltd.
1663 Liberty Drive
Bloomington, IN 47403   USA
www.authorhouse.co.uk
Phone: 0800.197.4150

Published by AuthorHouse 10/17/2013

ISBN: 978-1-4918-8198-9 (sc)
ISBN: 978-1-4918-8199-6 (e)

Contents

The Early Years 1

The In-Between Years 5

The Journey Begins 16

Reiki Healing 39

Travelling Tales 45

My Dogs 63

Stranger Than Fiction 77

UFOs 87

So What Happened to David? 91

Past Lives 94

Contacts 99

About the Author and the Book 101

Often when people meet a medium, they think he or she can read their mind and know everything about them. This is so untrue. Others think mediums know the answer to all their problems. Again this is untrue. We are just ordinary people having experience in this world to progress our soul. This is my journey.

www.wellingtonwitch.co.uk

The Early Years

I look around the room at the people sitting in my circle. We are just going to go off for a fifteen-minute meditation. I wonder where their paths will take them and who they will meet. This is the starting point of an exciting journey for them. They are at the very beginning of their development. My advice to them is to "sit still and listen"—not to me, but to their spirit guides. They settle down, follow the breathing exercise, and eventually start to relax. I have a look around and check that all are settled and safe.

My mind goes back over my own life and the things that have bought me to where I am today as well as the things that have shaped my life—some good, some not so good, but all experience.

I was born in a small town in the Black Country and am fiercely proud of being a black-country "wench". My family consisted of myself, an older sister, Mom, and Dad. My mom comes from a long line of spiritualists, clairvoyants, and witches. Dad's family is from Romany stock. They were powerful herbal healers. All these things were openly accepted and discussed within the family as normal, so I suppose I was lucky that when I spoke of the things I saw and heard as a child, it wasn't too worrying for my parents. The spirit world has been all around me for as long as I can remember. Mom tells me that I didn't walk or talk till I was two years old, but I was heard talking and laughing when alone in my room. Of course, I was speaking to the spirit world, my constant companions. I realise now that the people who came to me on a regular basis were my spirit guides.

A spirit guide is a positive entity who is here to help and guide you through your life on earth. Spirit guides are usually part of a past life, and they can change as your life changes, or they can stay with you throughout your life. It is usual to have more than one; five is usual. Most people go through life not even knowing of their existence, but when people start to develop their spiritual life, the first thing they want to learn about is spirit guides. They are not allowed to interfere with our journey on earth, but communicating with them can be very useful to help us make the right decisions, especially in times of crisis, and they can help us with our spiritual development.

All this was a normal part of my everyday life, so I grew up thinking that everyone saw the things and people from the spirit world as I did. My sister, on the other hand, had no interest in the spirit world, and as she got older, she was very outspoken, saying that everything that can't be proved scientifically is rubbish. She often told me that I would be locked up in an institution for some of the things I talked about. Mom has recently told me that she began to get worried about me as time went on, and she often spoke to Dad of her worries regarding my interest in the spirit world. Neither of my parents could see or hear spirits, so I can understand that my conversation with what appeared to be no one would indeed cause concern!

Life was good, and I had a very happy childhood. I have been told many times that I was a happy child, never bad-tempered and never asked for anything. I was content with my life and, of course, my spirit friends.

In those days all the children would play in the street: roller skating, cycling, and skipping. It was really an ordinary childhood. My playmates often asked about the people I saw and what they had to say. It was all like a game to them, I suppose.

My friends knew I loved animals, and if an injured animal was found, it always seemed to end up at our house. Mom and Dad were used to opening the door to a child bringing a frog or mouse that was injured for me to look after. I would pick leaves from the hedgerow to make a dressing for the injury. Nowadays I seem to have forgotten what to use. Perhaps these were genetic memories from my grandparents or before?

One day when I was about eight, I decided to have a garden sale to raise money for animal charities. This was the start of supporting animal charities that has carried on throughout my life. Back then, I sold anything—broken toys, plaster Paris models that I had painted, even the ones that were broken were sold as chalk. At Christmas I went carol singing to collect money for the dogs' home. Thinking about it, with my voice they must have paid me to shut up to go away!

One negative thing I remember is premonitions. Often I would wake up and feel uneasy and worried for no reason. My guides would come close and tell me not to worry. I was picking up an event that would happen very soon. I didn't understand, and for years I thought that I had actually caused the event, which was usually an earthquake, a plane crash, or something else that was linked to a large loss of life. I didn't like these feelings and always felt better once the event had happened. This added to my guilty feeling that it was my fault. Talking to people now, I realise that many sensitive people had similar experiences and feelings of guilt.

Of course, there were very positive sides to my contact with spirits as well. My friends were always keen to ask whom they would marry. Would they be rich? Would they be famous? I can clearly remember those long sunny days, watching the clouds roll across the blue sky and giving readings via their shape. Years later I realised that anything can be used as a tool to give readings. Not only cards and tea leaves but anything—including clouds!

As I got older I became very interested in the moon and the phases of the moon. I knew different phases made me feel different. When it was a new moon, I felt restless and wanted to start projects. A full moon made me want to be outside in the light of the moon and sit and think, while a waning moon made me want to clear things out of my life and tie up loose ends. My family mentioned that my interest in herbs and my close connection with the earth herself were common in the family, especially among the witches in the family. So was I a witch? What makes a witch? How do you know? I had always spent a lot of time with my nan, and we started talking about family and witchcraft at every opportunity. Slowly I learnt a lot of things about witchcraft, and by the age of fifteen I had a good understanding of my gifts and how I wanted to learn more.

The In-Between Years

The years rolled by, and very soon it was 1965. I was fifteen and anxious to leave school and start earning some money. I had been taking lessons at night school to learn shorthand and typing. It wasn't my ideal job, but at this point I had no idea what I wanted to be or do. All I knew was that I wanted to leave school and get on with life.

Seeing a job advertised in Birmingham, which was seven miles away, I took a day off school and went to an interview. The job was with a wholesale tobacconist. They wanted a copy typist, and to my surprise I was offered the job at a grand salary of three pounds, two shillings, and sixpence a week. The bus fare was going to be one pound a week, but who cares, I had a job! The school didn't see it that way, and I had detention for taking a day off.

So I started working in the red-light area of Birmingham. That sounds bad! I should say the company was located in the red-light area. My parents had no idea of this, and I never told them. Working there was certainly going to open my eyes to life. The company had a large staff of Irish Catholic employees. Why they took on an English witch I don't know; they must have been desperate. It was a very happy place to work, and I made many friends. One lady in particular was quite strange to look at, as she had no nose, or at least a very misshapen one. I felt a closeness to her, and one day she told me she was a direct descendant of Old Mother Shipton, a well-known witch in England. Maybe witches can recognise each other or know who else is a witch.

Meeting her led me to start looking around and trying to find out if there were any other witches in the area. I found out about a coven which met not too far away from where I worked. There were about fifteen in total in the group. I knew nothing about covens, and I just went along with what they said and where they went. They were of mixed ages and sexes, and I felt no real closeness to them, but I thought that maybe this was the right thing to do, to meet other witches. On the next full moon, they told me they were all meeting in a woodland area a few miles away and I could join them if I wanted to. Excited by the idea of actually being part of a coven, I happily went along. When we arrived, it was about 9.30 p.m., and there was loud music playing. The cars had all been parked in a circle, and some had the headlights on. There was a lot of drinking, and after a short time people started taking off their clothes. Very soon after that it seemed they were having sex with anyone and everyone. I wasn't prepared for this and made my excuses and left. If this was what witches did, then maybe I wasn't a witch after all. Looking back, I doubt they were even interested in the craft but were just looking for an excuse to be naked in the woods and have a lot of sex! It did put me off covens and groups though, and I have never since sought out groups for witches or covens and prefer to work as a solitary for esbats and sabbats (full moons and witches festivals). I am a solitary and a very happy solitary, thank you!

Never being a very good typist, I found the work I was doing a bit painful. I typed with my two index fingers on a Monday, used the next two on a Tuesday, worked with the ring fingers on a Wednesday, struggled on a Thursday, and was buggered by Friday when I had to go back to my painful index fingers.

One day the boss told me I was to learn how to use the switchboard. It looked daunting, with lights and a lot of cords that all seemed to be twisted around each other. There was also an internal telephone system and a tannoy. Oh no! I was never going to use that! So I had my lessons from the lady in charge. She said, "Okay, you can answer the next call."

For what seemed like hours, I sat there willing it not to ring. I was hot and sweaty and terrified. Then the little flap on the switchboard dropped, and I heard the familiar ring, ring, ring. Oh no, I had a call!

"Go on, answer it then."

"What shall I say?"

"Ask them what they want."

So I plugged in and said, "What do you want?" It had to be the boss on the other end, didn't it? He demanded to know who I was and why I hadn't answered correctly. Luckily, I got away with it. A good job as a telephonist was to be my career for the next forty years. After I got the hang of it, I loved it, and I never had to use the dreaded typewriter again.

The switchboard was from the 1920s and was called a 10x50 PBX. It could be very temperamental, and some days the staff would hear me scream and would find me in a heap behind the door as I suffered yet another electric shock when the metal on the end of the cords made contact with the metal rings on my fingers.

In the early days I said I would never use the tannoy system, but I soon found it was my best friend, especially when I had an irate customer on the phone asking for a member of staff whom I couldn't find. The workplace consisted of a warehouse and showroom with offices above. Next door was an old spit-and-sawdust pub, and next door to that was our head office. It was a very strange set up. Usually when people couldn't be found in the warehouse or office, a quick shout on the tannoy managed to find them in the pub, swearing as they ran back to their desk that they had been in the loo. The joint managing directors were very old school. Women were not allowed to wear trousers even in the cold weather, and there were a lot more rules that people would laugh at today. One of the MDs was ex-RAF, and he had a tannoy in his office that overruled mine. Often I would be in mid flow when his voice boomed out, "Mr Jones, to my office! Scramble!" I am sure he still thought the war was on.

One day I was asked to take some company money to the bank a few streets away. A car came up close, and the driver asked me directions. As I bent down to talk to him, I realised he was naked. As I made a hasty getaway, the ladies leaning out of the windows advertising their wares had a good laugh. On another occasion I remember I asked a lad I knew to drive down the main road where the ladies of the night touted for business. We were in his van, myself and a friend hiding in the back. I'm not sure why I asked. I suppose it sounded like a laugh at the time. At the top end of the road he asked one lady, "How much?"

"Ten pounds."

As we drove further down the street, it got cheaper and cheaper, till at the other end we found a young girl, who was probably about sixteen. She eyed the lad up and down, smiled, and said, "Ten shillings." He shook his head and was verbally abused by the girl.

"What do you think? This is bloody charity week?"

Often on my early-morning journey to work, as I got closer to the office, I would see people lying in the road close to some of the seedy clubs, some with hangovers, some bruised and beaten. It became common to see these things; it was a good thing my parents never found out what sort of an area I was working in. My sister worked at an accountant's, and one day she was working close by. She asked if we could meet for lunch and turned up to meet me with a male colleague. The owner of the café was eyeing her up and asked her work colleague if she was his wife. He blushed and said, "No, she's my boss." The café owner then looked at me and asked if I was his wife. Again he shook his head, and the café owner then asked how much we were . . .

In 1965 we were right in the middle of the swinging sixties, a great time to be a teenager. There was great music and fun everywhere. At this time many people were experimenting with drugs. One night at a party I was talking to a girl who had taken LSD. She was smiling and was saying, "Lyn, you have lovely pretty colours around you. Oh, look at him! Oh, it's so lovely!" Hmmm, people have colours around them? Yes, I know we do. Another claimed he was hearing voices talking to him, and there didn't appear to be anyone nearby. Yes, of course, the spirit world talked to us all the time. One poor girl was in a state of shock. She could see loads of people in the room and was terrified because no one else could see them. I remember thinking, "What's wrong with these people? It's all quite normal."

Later on that evening at home, I picked up the book I was reading. It was all about the human aura and was written by a Tibetan monk. As I thumbed through the pages, I read a sentence that changed my life. It said that not many people could actually see the aura and that not everyone saw spirits or spoke to guides and people from the spirit world.

What? So at the tender age of fifteen the penny finally dropped. It was I who was odd. No one probably had a clue what I had been on about all these years. At fifteen I wanted to be the same as everyone else, so I said I would never use these gifts again. I worked hard at turning them off and closing them down. The more I pushed them away, the more ill I felt. I was nervous, stressed, and physically ill. I lost count of the times my parents took me to see a doctor, who said I was suffering from nervous tension and exhaustion. One doctor, having seen me three times in one week, threw down his stethoscope and said, "You tell me what's wrong, because I can't find anything wrong with you!" He told my parents that if I couldn't help myself, then I might have to have psychiatric help.

All of this was happening at the same time that the company I worked for was being taken over. The new company suddenly cut the staff by three quarters, so as well as operating a very busy 10x50 PBX switchboard, I was taking orders by phone, doing accounts, chasing problems, and some days even putting orders together in the warehouse. My health was getting worse. I know now that, apart from the stress, I was starting to suffer from OCD, and it was taking over my life. Every day I felt that, if I didn't carry out various rituals in the same order every day, something terrible would happen. This went on for a while, until one day I called for a telecom engineer to mend my switchboard, as my usual silver paper and nail file couldn't fix the problem this time! He told me that the GPO (which is now BT) needed operators in their office in Birmingham. I applied for a job and was lucky enough to start work with them. With a different scene and less stress, I felt a bit better, but I was always nervy and on edge.

The work was great, and the switch room was huge, with over 1,500 10x50 PBX switchboards in one place. I loved working there, especially the 999 calls. No two days were the same, and the training I received was excellent. Sadly, though, the journey from home to work was taking longer every day as the volume of traffic increased and the city grew bigger an busier.

I was offered a job in my home town as a telephonist, and not having the two-hour journey twice a day was wonderful. It was around this time that my mom wanted to visit the spiritualist church in a town near where we lived and asked if I would I go with her. So off we went— Mom, Dad, and myself. Dad wasn't keen on coming with us and spent the whole journey fooling about and joking about the meeting we were going to. I can remember him looking up at the sky and shouting, "Uncle Bill, come on down!" Mom and I, although amused, told him not to joke about it. We parked and walked into the church where we quietly sat in the back row as all newcomers try to do.

The medium looked at me and smiled. Some of the committee also looked at me and smiled. Wow! I instinctively knew they were the same as me. I just knew they could see and hear spirits as I could. I wasn't odd. I was normal. Well, maybe normal is going too far, as my husband said when he read this bit."

The medium started her clairvoyance and asked if she could go to my dad and pass on a message. When she said she had Uncle Bill to speak to him, Mom and I both had to stifle a giggle after his come-on-down jokes in the car! The evidence was first class. After Uncle Bill, she brought through a lot of Dad's army friends from the war. It was excellent evidence, and she said to Dad, "You're a disbeliever, aren't you?"

He nodded.

"Well, do you believe now?"

"No."

Mom and I both gave him a glare. To say he was a disbeliever is a bit harsh. He had his beliefs, and he supported us in our beliefs. He said he had never seen a spirit but would believe if he saw one. One of his favourite sayings was "Believe nothing you hear and half of what you see." He told us of a time when he was a teenager and had been to the cinema to see Frankenstein and Dracula on together as a double bill. Taking a shortcut home through the fields, he heard chains rattling and saw a white figure moving about. Having been scared by the film, he turned around and ran the long way back home. The next day his fear had turned to curiosity, so he went back to the fields and laughed when he saw that his "ghost" was a nanny goat chained to a stake to graze.

After the service I was elated because I had found a lot of other people like me. From that day I made a promise to the spirits that I would use my gifts and help as many people as I could throughout my life. I hope that I have kept that promise and will be able to do so for a long time to come.

Time moved on, and eventually I met a man at work. We married and had two children. My boys became the most important thing in my life. The relationship with my husband was never very good, and we both knew it had been a mistake to get married, but we stayed together for a few years.

One day my guides told me, "It's a very important time for you. You have free will and can stay as you are, or you can learn and experience what you came to earth to do. Remember, it's what you chose before you were born. If you have changed your mind, you can do so." These words didn't mean much to me, and I was puzzled by what they meant.

As I have said, my marriage wasn't happy, and I thought that if I could go back to work, I would have more to think about and could earn some much-needed money as well. A few weeks later, a large supermarket was opening in our town. I saw they needed people to stock shelves. I applied, filled out the application form, and waited. Not long afterwards I had a phone call from the company asking if I would be interested in a part-time evening and Saturday job as a telephonist/telex operator due to my past training. This would fit in well with the children, so I said yes. I was back in the working community and had all day with my boys.

The staff started work and had training before the store officially opened, and on the third day we were encouraged to walk around and see where various departments were and meet the other staff. I walked into the photography and electrical department and stopped dead in my tracks. There was a man who introduced himself as deputy manager of the department. I will refer to him as David (not his real name). As we shook hands and our eyes met, I felt a shockwave go through me like electricity. We stood looking at each other and holding hands for what seemed like an eternity. It was as though I was meeting myself. I knew that he would understand all the things that I did and saw.

From that day on I couldn't wait to get to work. David would phone me whenever the department was quiet, and we started meeting up in the daytime when his shift pattern allowed. We talked about everything. It was all so easy to talk to him. As the weeks passed, I found out that he was married and had a son, but the marriage was over and he was living back with his parents. He was originally from a small place near Nairobi in East Africa and had Indian parents. His parents were well-to-do in Africa. His father worked for a tea company, and his mother was a former beauty queen. They had made the decision to bring him and his sister to England for their education, and they had been in the United Kingdom since 1958. In Africa they had lived in a large house with servants and had enjoyed a very good life. He told me that he was born on October 13 in 1952 at midnight during a thunderstorm. The local spiritual people told his mom that it was an omen, that he was a very spiritual person, and that he would need special protection, as the dark side would try to stop him working at every opportunity.

One day a servant was taking him to school. It was hot, and the sun was casting shadows. He noticed they were following a lady who was carrying a bundle of food or something similar on her head. He thought that something didn't look right. At the same moment the servant must have noticed the same thing as they looked at the figure before them. They noticed her feet were pointing in the wrong direction and that she cast no shadow as she walked. Quickly the servant picked him up and ran all the way back to the house with him. We were never sure if this incident had anything to do with the family decision to move or if the move really was for education.

Since he had been in the United Kingdom, he told me, he had had no real beliefs. He was interested in a lot of things and was still searching for answers. His father had kept his Hindu beliefs, while his mother and sister had become Jehovah's Witnesses. You can imagine the conversation at meal times were "different" to say the least, with me throwing in my witch's opinion whenever possible!

Leaving my children's father and setting up home with a new partner didn't go down well with anyone. My family stopped speaking to me, and I lost touch with all my friends. We both lost our jobs due to company policy, so we were at rock bottom. We moved into a beautiful flat. I was worried about how we would pay for it. He said something would turn up, and I believed him.

The Journey Begins

Even with the family difficulties, I wanted to be with David twenty-four hours a day. We had nothing at all except our belief that destiny had brought us together for a reason. We became interested in reading any books about spiritual beliefs, ghosts, UFOs, or ascended masters. In fact, we read constantly for six months. One name kept cropping up all of the time—St Germain. We were both drawn to his teachings and couldn't read enough about him. One day when I was reading about the philosopher's stone, something stirred in the back of my mind. I knew this. As I said earlier, I was aware of spirits and my guides from an early age, and one in particular who always appeared to me when I asked for help. He gave very good advice, and I loved his words of wisdom. He was called Germain, not "Saint", just Germain. Was it possible that I had been working with the ascended master Germain all these years? The easiest thing to do was ask, but as usual his answer was not a straight yes or no. I was aware that when we ask questions we don't get yes or no answers. We have free will, and spirits can't interfere unless we ask them to. Even then they won't tell us what to do; instead they will guide us.

"I am known by many names," he replied. "I have had many lives on earth. I will teach you much more in the coming years. I have walked beside you for many years and will always be by your side." He always appeared to me as a man about thirty-five years old, usually dressed in a modern suit or loose clothes, and usually his clothes had a hint of violet, either the shirt or the robe. He sometimes had a short goatee beard and was sometimes clean shaven. This picture in the book looked nothing like him—but the twinkle in his eyes was the same!

Time moved on, and it was almost Christmas. I celebrated the December 21 winter solstice and Yule. Christmas is always exciting for children, and we wanted all of our three children to have gifts. We decided to go to a nearby pawn shop and pawn our wedding rings and a necklace he had from his family. We were offered £75, a fortune after having no money for months. We found that, try as we might, we couldn't bring ourselves to spend any of it. After catching the bus back to our home town, I was feeling very sad and lonely. I missed the family a lot, but they still didn't want to know us. I wanted to see them, so I made my way to my old childhood home. It was getting dark, and I could see everyone in the front room laughing and enjoying themselves as I had done with them for so many Christmases in the past. That was probably one of the lowest ebbs I can remember. I was standing on the outside of everything I wanted to be part of and was only able to look through the window. They had no idea I was so close and yet so far away.

Germain told us many things, and we continued to read any books we could get hold of about his work on earth. A mystery man to be sure! One story intrigued us. In one part of the world a disc was made of half lead and half gold. There was no join to see, and it was supposed to have been turned to pure gold by Germain. Maybe we could make gold from lead and get out of debt?

It seems silly now, but we were convinced that together we could achieve anything. We had no lead or gold, only a silver 1923 sixpence to experiment with, as pre 1923 coins were made of silver not with any added base metals. So we boiled the sixpence with some mercury! As it boiled, it glowed golden, and we thought that we had succeeded in making gold. We were so over-excited that we left the pan boiling, and it set fire to the kitchen blinds and worktop. Not good, and when it cooled down the coin was as black as the ace of spades. The landlord didn't share our enthusiasm, so we were on the move again, as we were asked to leave the flat. So where to now?

We were doing our best to make ends meet and only hitting brick walls. We were trying really hard to make a living, and as he had a decent camera, we tried taking wedding photos, portraits, and animal pictures. One day we were asked to take some photographs to make up a portfolio for a man who had started a business building stone fireplaces. I was trusted to do this by myself, as David didn't think I could make a mess of a fireplace, so I went alone. I explained to the customer that I had no car and needed a lift. All went well until the last picture, which had to be taken several miles away. We got into the van and started making conversation. I asked how long he had been doing this work.

"Six months."

"What did you do before?"

"Nothing. I was in prison."

It was one of those moments where your mouth runs away with you, and without thinking I said, "What did you do?"

"I killed my wife."

I felt the protection of my spirit guides as they whispered, "It's fine. You're safe." I still cringe when I think of the next thing I said.

"Oh well, she probably deserved it" came out of my mouth. We sat in silence for the rest of the journey.

David was a very talented photographer, artist, and sculptor. In fact, he was very good at anything he tried. We still couldn't get on and were beginning to wonder what to do. His dad said maybe we could go and stay with his brother, who had recently bought a house and shop in London. We could stay there where there were so many job opportunities. With no developments with my family, I decided we had nothing to lose, so we moved to London.

While living at the small shop and flat, we often visited another uncle. He was quite an imposing figure, highly respected by the rest of the family, and was called "Number One". I was told he was involved in the black magic. This scared me a lot, as I had no real understanding and had had no contact with black magic at that time. I always tried to make excuses for not staying at his house. One night we missed the bus home and were invited to stay. I dreamt that a huge slug crawled onto the bed and was about to attack me, and in my dream I hit out at it and beat it with a walking stick I saw lying on the bedroom floor. Waking up in a panic and a hot sweat, I was relieved it was a dream. Imagine my surprise and fear the next day when number one uncle was limping badly and claimed to have fallen down the stairs. Maybe he could shape shift and had become the slug in my dream?

Another thing I remember is when the whole family hired the local town hall for a family celebration to mark the birth of a new child into the family. Six hundred people were invited. I heard a lot of shouting and arguing in their own language. As neither David nor I spoke the language, we had little idea what was wrong until one young girl looked at me and said, "Some of the family won't go because of you." It was a shock to realise they didn't want me there as I was not Indian—and I was a witch!

From day one I hated living in London. The only good thing was that there were a lot of jobs. I got a job as a temp with an agency and had so much work to choose from. David was working in a photography shop, so at least we had money coming in. He was also meeting a lot of people who loved his photography and art. We had the chance to go to the United States with a well-known band to cover their tour photographically. We were to pay our own airfare, which was impossible. I wonder where that might have led?

Our spiritual research had led us to believe that one of the museums in London had some artefacts that were found in the pyramids. One was a ball of light that didn't seem to have any source from which the light came, and the other was a tube of light similar to the light sabre in *Star Wars*. We went along to the museum and asked to see them. We were fobbed off and told there were no such things. A few minutes later we were approached by another member of staff and escorted from the premises and told never to return as we were trouble-makers!

In one way these were exciting times, but on the other hand we were not as happy as we had been in the Midlands. One night we were walking along a road close to where we lived, and a gang of teenagers came up behind us and overtook us. They then slowed down so that we had to overtake them. They started shouting racial abuse and said that people like "him" had no right to walk on the same road as them. It got very nasty, and after a lot of pushing and shoving, I heard one of my guides say, "Beware!" As he spoke, I saw the glint of steel and realized that one of them had pulled a knife. He lifted his arm to stab David, and I put my arm up to protect him as he was pushed to the ground. I suddenly felt a sharp pain and realised the knife had gone straight through my hand. I screamed as the blood poured out, and the gang moved back. We made our way back to the flat, but they followed us. They broke in and severely beat up David.

This wasn't at all what I had thought our life together was going to be like. Everything seemed to be going wrong. A short while ago as a couple we had felt invincible, People noticed us and seemed to remember us as a couple everywhere we went. Now everything was different, and we started disagreeing on a lot of things. I was very unhappy in London and wondered what to do.

As I said, I was working as a temp at the time. One day they sent me to a gold-bullion dealer. I was just getting the hang of the job and learning who was who, when a manager asked me to push a button on the wall. I turned round from my switchboard and pushed the button. The switchboard was very busy, so I carried on with my work. All hell broke loose, and suddenly it was like a film set. People were running around, and a man stood in front of me with a gun! He said, "No one move!" You have to be joking! I was far too scared to breathe, never mind move. Then everything went back to normal, and the man with the gun apologised. The button was a raid warning to Scotland Yard. It had to be kept quiet or no one would take any notice and treat it as the test that it was.

Enough is enough. I rang the agency, and they sent me to another job in a different suburb. One of the girls I worked with was lovely. She said she had a husband who was working in Somerset. He was an engineer and was working on a big project in a small town. She had a flat close by and invited us to stay for a few days. Her cousin was staying there as well. On the first night we were watching TV, and I noticed a mist was filling the room. It hovered about six inches from the floor. I was scared and asked the spirits what was happening. They told me to leave the flat at once. At that moment the TV went blank, and a voice came over the TV.

"Do not try to fight us. You have no chance. Join us, and you will have more treasures than you ever thought possible. Fight us and be destroyed."

As quick as it had happened, it all went back to normal. I was scared and asked my guides what it was about. They said that it was the dark side trying to get us to join them. I had never heard of the dark side. What was it and why could it give us treasures? The thoughts haunted me all night, and I was relieved the next day when I could get out of there.

Around this time the film *The Exorcist* came out. We went to see it, and although I wasn't afraid, I did insist on having the lights on for three weeks at bedtime.

David's dad told us that he had witnessed a real exorcism in Africa in his own family. His sister had upset a local witch doctor by pointing at his house and laughing at the state of it. He was supposed to have cursed her. Soon after this, she started having fits. As I have said before, the family was wealthy, so she had access to all the best medical treatment. Nothing was ever found to have caused the fits. One day a stranger came through the village. He said she was cursed and needed to be exorcised. The whole family had to be present. All doors and windows had to be secured. He said there would be a risk to the girl. If the spirit possessing her was strong, she would run to him. That would mean she would die. He started the exorcism by chanting and saying prayers. He burnt herbs and chanted some more. After an hour he said that the girl was weak and he had to give her a rest. As he stopped chanting, she ran to the locked door. She ripped out all of her nails by scratching the woodwork to get out. They brought her back and started again. This time a lighted candle flame was put inside her mouth. A voice was heard from somewhere inside her body saying, "Stop it. You're burning me." The exorcist asked the spirit to leave the girl. He eventually said he would. This went on for several hours, until at last the man was satisfied the spirit had left. The girl was fine after that, but the exorcist told the family she had to wear some elephant-tail hair around her arm that could never be taken off and could never got wet. It was made for her and bound with gold. She wore it just above her elbow. After this her health improved. She had no more fits, and in later years she went to university and eventually became a doctor. I met her some years later in the United Kingdom, and what I remember most were her eyes; they had no light, no warmth, no soul.

Things went from bad to worse with David and me. I decided to go back to the Midlands and pick up the pieces of my life. When I rang my family and said we were no longer together, they said I would be welcome to go home. So I went back to my parents' house.

Having two young children, I wanted the best for them, so I decided to make a complete new start. After very little thought and with no planning to how all this would work out, I decided to go to New Street train station in Birmingham. I would trust that the spirits would help me to be where I should be. I would get the first train to arrive and start a new life there. The first train was a Plymouth train. I only had enough money to go part of the journey. Looking back, I realise that anything could have gone wrong. I had utter trust in the spirits. They had always been there with me, and so I trusted them.

The train came to a halt at a station. Having never been there before, I wandered around the platform looking for the exit. I saw a local newspaper lying on a bench. Reading through it, I saw that a local company wanted a telephonist. The name of the town sounded familiar. Wasn't it mentioned that night in the flat—the night of my first encounter with the dark side? I was sure it was the same place. I rang the number and was told to get a bus to the next town and then ask for directions. When I got off the bus, I walked down a narrow alley and was surprised to see the company I was looking for soon come into sight.

Everyone was busy, and I was left in reception. There was a man trying to operate the switchboard. He looked very hassled. He was muttering about this new-fangled contraption. I looked and smiled. It was a new type of switchboard that I had operated many times in London.

"Can you work this?" he asked.

"Yes."

"Well come over here and do it then."

So three hours later, I was still operating the switchboard when the personnel manager came to find me. She had forgotten I was there. The elderly gentleman told her to hire me, as I was able to sort out this confounded monster.

I was told that there was a lady in the town who ran a small boarding house. I booked myself in for three nights, which would take me to the weekend. Finding somewhere to live was difficult. The only place I could find was a flat in the next town. It was run down and shabby but affordable.

David, whom I now considered my ex-partner, was still very much in tune with me and found me in a few days. He told me he missed me and that he wanted us to be together. The spark was still as strong as ever, so we decided to get back together For a short while it was good. Looking back, I can see now that he had already been seduced by the dark side. He got a job, and we found a flat nearer to where we worked, but his behaviour became erratic and strange. He became even more jealous and aggressive. I was scared of him and even more scared to leave. My work colleagues were used to seeing me turn up for work with a black eye or a badly bruised arm. Of course, I never let on what had happened, but they must have known.

We were still taking photographs for weddings and any doing other photographic work that came up. We were approached by a man called Jamie (name changed) from a local club. They wanted some large black and white photographs of old scenes of the town to put in a new hall they were building. There was a huge attraction between Jamie and me. He was kind and seemed to know I was having a difficult life with my partner. He said I should leave, as I would be better off on my own, but I was too scared of what would happen to me after the beatings I had received for doing nothing. So I stayed where I was for now. Strangely enough, around this time I also met the man who was to become my husband, but we were not destined to be married for another twenty-two years. He and his wife had just had a son, and they wanted me to take the christening photographs. How things twist and turn. That child is now my step-son!

Time went on. I bought a car, and on July 7 1977 (7.7.77) David and I got married. Probably because the date was unique, the story made front-page news in the local newspaper, with pictures of us looking happy. Some times were good, but there was always the underlying feeling that at any time he could snap. Several times I found him surrounded by cans of cider and beer and an empty bottle of pills. Once I hesitated before calling the ambulance. If he was dead, we would be free. My guides encouraged me to call the ambulance as I didn't want that on my conscience. Whenever he did this, he admitted he was very unhappy. He wanted to work for the light but also wanted the power and wealth from the dark side. He promised to change, and each time it lasted about two weeks before he would revert back to the violent person I feared.

Years later I was to work with women who had been in circumstances similar to those I had been in at this time, and they always said the same things. He didn't mean it. He promised never to do it again. I know how easy it is to fall for this chat, as I had heard it myself so many times.

The spirit world was encouraging me to use my gifts to help people and to start meeting spiritual people like myself. I started doing clairvoyant one-on-one readings, and I was surprised that people were interested in what I could tell them. This deepened my love of working for the spirits, and I knew without a doubt this was to be part of my life always.

David, on the other hand, was intrigued by the dark side. He started carrying out rituals that I now know are black magic. He told me that he had a hold on my soul and that I would never escape him. The jealousy and violence became so bad that I was forever in a state of fear. He would stand by the door and wait for me to come back from work. He had timed it. It should take twelve minutes to walk home, not thirteen or fifteen, but twelve. Anything else led to an inquest. "Where have you been? Who did you speak to?" This could go on for as much as six hours. The stress was unbearable. My weight dropped to five stone ten. It didn't help that I only ate every other day. David kept all the money, so I had to go without so that the boys would always have food.

One night on my way home I met Jamie. I was always happy to see him, and it probably showed. He told me he would still be willing to help me to leave David. I didn't realise that David was standing by the doorway and saw me talking to Jamie. As I walked through the door I was met by a punch in the face that broke a cheek bone. A kick from his army boots broke several ribs. I was hysterical and ran outside to escape. He caught me and dragged me back indoors by my hair. Then he said I was a mess and dragged me to the bathroom to wash the blood off. He slammed my head into the wash basin and knocked out a tooth. Then he went round the flat with a hammer and scissors. He broke or cut up every single thing that was mine. Now I had nothing but the clothes that I was wearing. He pushed me down the stairs and casually stepped over me, before going out and locking me in. I lay there for a whole day before I was able to drag myself upstairs. I was locked in for a week until the bruises faded.

Friends urged me to tell the truth about what had happened and to leave. I was a regular at the local hospital, where I was known by name. Whether it was bruising or being pushed through a door or window, the injuries became more frequent. One day I knew I was in for it. We had gone out, and someone had upset him. He started drinking, and I recognised the signs. Terrified to be alone with him, I faked an illness and begged him to take me to a doctor. The doctor asked me what was wrong. I made up all sorts of stories. I had a headache, a stomach ache, pins and needles in my fingers, and so on. He looked at me. I was crying out inside, and my eyes were pleading with him to help me. He seemed to know I needed help, but unless I was honest he could do nothing, so he had to send me home.

Things got much worse. I started sleeping with a carving knife under my pillow, and I know that if David had hit me again while I had the knife close by, I would have killed him. In the meantime he could have easily killed me in one of his drunken rages.

The turning point came one day when I popped out to the shop for a bottle of milk. I was gone five minutes, and when I walked in, I found that he had attacked my youngest son with a garden cane and badly marked his back, leaving welts and bruises. This was the first time he had ever touched the boys, and it was the last. I grabbed the boys and left, taking nothing except what we were wearing. Through stinging tears and in terror of the future, we drove, not aware of where we were going, but I knew without a doubt that we were now free. Having nowhere to go, we lived in the car for two weeks. I heard that David had gone back to the Midlands to live with his mother after losing our flat and his job. Recently I had the chance to re-visit the house where the abuse happened and lay a few ghosts to rest. This helped me a lot.

I missed my friends in Somerset, and one day I rang Jamie and asked if we were all still welcome to stay with him. We stayed together for the next eleven years. He helped me to heal emotionally and physically, and I will always be grateful for the kindness and the sanctuary he gave us when we needed help. We are still good friends even though we have both moved on.

Life became quiet and relaxed, with no drama and no problems. I was working for an employment agency, and one of the first jobs they sent me to was as a telephonist at the very same company my London friend's husband worked for. The position was for two weeks. I loved it and was sorry it would only be for two weeks. Well, they must have forgotten all about me. I stayed there for the next twenty-four years. At home we did the usual family things—holidays and family visits. It was a very happy time. I had quite a collection of people for whom I did readings, and I started attending the spiritualist church a few miles away.

Looking back, I think things started to change around 1987. I had a feeling of restlessness, a strange feeling that I needed to do something—but what? I asked my guides, and they said I must follow my heart. There were no signs of anything I was particularly drawn to, so I was at a loss as to what I ought to be doing. Three years later I hit forty and felt the need to run away. I was not sure what I thought that would achieve, but run away I did. I went to stay with a friend. I did a lot of thinking. I realised that

I was forty and had very little to show for my years on earth. I wanted something of my own, a desire to achieve something. I was happy and settled with Jamie. He hadn't done anything wrong, and I couldn't explain what these feelings were. I just felt that I needed to be doing something.

Although I was working as a telephonist every day, I joined a voluntary organisation that helps people in crisis. This filled a gap for a short while. I still felt I hadn't found what I was looking for. The feelings got much stronger, until one day my guides told me "it was time". Time for what? Time to step out and be me, they said. This was very hard, as there was simply no reason to up sticks and move out.

The feeling to move on was strong, so I counted how much money I had in the bank and made a decision to buy a house. My oldest son was now twenty-one, and we got a joint mortgage. I provided the deposit, and we bought a house. My youngest son moved in as well. I was still not sure what the spirits wanted me to do, but for now I was happy in the knowledge that this was my house. I could be safe and happy here with my family, and I could wait to see what the spirits had planned for me.

Things changed one day when a young man walked into my reception area at work. He peered around the doorway and asked if we had any jobs. At the same time we smiled and said in unison, "It's you!" This was Jak. He came in, and although I had never met him before (not in this life anyway), it was as if we had known each other for many years. He eventually got a job with the company and moved in with us as a lodger. He was a very talented artist and musician, and although he was sixteen years younger than me, we soon became an item. Even though he was so much younger, he was so wise. He taught me more about myself in the eight years we were together than I had learnt in my whole life. Slowly I grew to like myself again, and I laughed out loud for the first time in years. He felt like my soul mate, and he was my salvation. One of the things he taught me was that if you really love someone, you must not hang on to them tightly or you will crush the love to death. Open your hand and let it grow. I am a Taurus, and he is an Aries. Sometimes we would have a difference of opinion and lock horns. We never argued, but we were both stubborn. If this happened and no one would give in, he would disappear to the shops for cream cakes. His philosophy was that you have to see the humour in any situation when your face is covered in cream!

It wasn't always sweetness and light, though, as you can imagine with a bull and a ram. One day he was helping me wash up. It was a bright sunny day, and the kitchen window was open in front of the sink. As I washed the dishes, he dried them. What I didn't notice was that he was then putting them back in the water and I was washing them over and over again. When I did notice, I was so angry that I pushed the whole lot through the window. They all fell and broke into dozens of pieces, and he went outside to clear up the mess. I had a saucepan in my hand and threw it at him, narrowly missing his head as he ducked at the precise moment. "Missed!" he said. To the day I sold that house it had the dent in the wall from the saucepan.

One cold winter day everyone had gone out. I thought I would light a log fire so that the house would be warm and cosy to come back to. I lit a firelighter from the gas cooker and started to walk to the next room with it to light the fire. It caught light to my sweater sleeve. I rushed to the sink and threw the firelighter into the sink. Missing the sink, it fell down the back of the sink unit and quickly set fire to the vinyl floor covering. Soon the flames were right up the window and had started to burn the window frame. Knowing there were a lot of cleaning fluids and aerosols under the sink, I swept them all out with the sweep of an arm. The dogs were terrified by the noise and the flames and fled upstairs onto the bed for safety. Grabbing a bowl and bucket, I filled them and threw the water down the back of the sink until I was sure the fire was out. After dismantling part of the cupboard to make sure it was clear of any fire, I realised I was paddling in about an inch of water. After sweeping most of it outside and mopping up the rest, I noticed my reflection in the mirror. My face was streaked with black smoke, and I was soaking wet. Once the house was back to normal I sat on the stairs and cried. Just then I heard the door open and everyone came in. Jak said, "It's a bit cold in here, I am surprised you didn't light the fire." If I had had a saucepan in my hand right them I wouldn't have missed!

I was very busy with clairvoyant reading, and I always had a houseful of people needing help. Christmas and Yule celebrations at the house were "open house". Anyone who had nowhere to go was welcome to join us. Luckily, we never had so many that we couldn't cope, and we always made room for as many as we could. Work at the church was also busy; I was learning so much about the spirit world and how I could use what gifts I was born with more efficiently. Life was good. Jak understood about witchcraft, spiritual contacts, guides, and the like, and we talked for hours and hours about the subject. I suppose it's true that people come into our life for a reason at the right time. He certainly came into my life to teach me how to learn to love myself again and how to love other people unconditionally.

I'm not sure if it was because of our age difference, or maybe our time together was done. We had taught and learnt all we needed to, and now we could continue with our own personal journeys. We stayed together for a while longer, but it was as friends, good friends, and we are still that to this day.

A few years later he was the best man at Roger's and my wedding. A few years before this, when we had realised that our relationship was more on a friendly basis than romantic, I went on holiday with a girlfriend to Jamaica. I will tell you more about this a bit later on. For now I want to tell you about a man I met there. It was my birthday, and my girlfriend and I had decided to mark the day by going skinny dipping. We found a quiet cove, took off all of our clothes, and jumped into the warm Caribbean. We were laughing and joking and hadn't noticed that two men were standing looking over the rocks.

"Get out of there," one of them shouted. "There is a storm coming!" I found out later this was Mike. We asked them to go away so we could get our clothes on. "Too late," they joked, "The sun's shining right through the water."

So nothing was left to the imagination! In our desperation to clamber out, my friend stood on a sea urchin, and the spines broke off in her foot. We dressed and went to meet the two men who had been watching us. My friend told them it was my birthday, and they gave us a can of beer to celebrate and invited us out for a meal that evening. In the meantime a local man had bought some black boot polish, telling my friend it was the cure for urchin spines. If she would smother the heel of her foot with it and cover it with a plaster, the spines would work their way out. Not at all sure about this, she tried it. She said it felt better, but she thought it was more likely to be the very large Bacardi and cola or the pain killers she had taken.

The meal went well, and we found out that the men we had met were on holiday there. Mike worked for Canadian Airlines, and his friend worked for American Airlines. They were staying at the same hotel as us, so later on we met them by the bar for a drink. My friend and I were in Jamaica for a rest and some sun; romance wasn't on the agenda. Mike said he had a really bad back and was on holiday from work for a rest. He lived in Canada. We started talking about things in general. He was interested in all spiritual things, and I asked if he wanted me to do any healing on his back. I had recently completed my training as a Reiki master. We talked right into the early hours. I told him that I lived with my sons and Jak, and I described my life with David. I informed him that my spiritual life and healing were now more important to me than relationships.

I had recently sold the last bits of jewellery left from my marriage to pay for the Reiki training. He asked if I wanted to go back to his room where maybe he could experience this Reiki. I hardly knew him. He was a lovely guy, but I declined the offer and said I would send him some distant healing. I think he took this as a rebuff, but I was true to my word, and when I was back in my room, I tuned into the healing energy and sent him love, light, and healing to his back.

The next day he was by the swimming pool early and couldn't wait to tell me he had felt the healing. "It was as if something was manipulating my back. It felt hot and all the pain was gone!"

"Good," I said and smiled.

He asked if I would like to go out with him, and I told him I wasn't interested in a relationship, so thanks, but no thanks. I don't think he was very happy with me. We exchanged addresses, and he was quite abrupt when he left later that day for the airport.

The holiday came to an end. It had been a great time, and it was with mixed feelings that we made the journey home. A few weeks later a letter arrived with a Canadian stamp on it. I read it and felt both shock and disbelief. It was from Mike. He said he had been living with a lady in Canada for seventeen years, but after meeting me he had realised that their relationship was over. He really wanted to see me, and would I meet up with him in England?

As he worked for the airline, he could travel easily and cheaply. We made arrangements to meet in Glastonbury. I booked a room at a hotel, and we met at an arranged place. It was almost like a blind date, as we both knew little about each other. The meeting was a huge success, although I thought it would be over before it started. When I found my room and opened the door, I became aware of a little dog from the spirit world. I was talking to it, and it jumped on the bed. Mike said he felt it jump on the bed and was a bit freaked out. Then I began talking to someone from the spirit world who had come through to give Mike a message. I described the person and told him the name. Luckily, he was very interested in all the things I do. Glastonbury was a very good choice to meet after all. He had told his mother in Canada that he had met a witch, who at this time had purple hair, tattoos, and a nose stud. She must have been very worried for her son! When I eventually met his mother we ended up good friends.

The next few years were a whirl of my trips to Canada and his to the United Kingdom. We made plans for me to go and live in Canada and even made arrangements to have crates made to take my beloved dogs with me. It was all so close, and yet . . . it didn't feel right. My guides were exceptionally quiet about the move. All they said was that I must follow my heart. Yes, I had learnt that from Jak. My heart wasn't really in the move. Things carried on like this for a few months. I always looked forward to our meetings. We had fun, but I always looked forward to being on my own again. That wasn't right, was it? If I was to move to Canada and spend 24/7 with this man, I had to be one hundred per cent sure.

I was thinking about all of this while I sat at my switchboard, when the man who mended my car came in. His name was Roger. Yes, the very same man I had done the christening photographs for all those years ago. He told me he was having a flat warming that night, and did I want to come? Mike was over from Canada, and I was due to take him to the airport at 4.00 p.m. I asked if Jak could come to the party as well, and he said, "Of course." So after putting Mike on the plane home, I went to the party. After a while I had a good look at who was there and asked Roger where his wife was. He told me they had split up quite a while before, and this was his new flat on his own. By the end of the evening we were getting on like a house on fire, and he asked me if I would like to go out the following Friday. I accepted. Well, a lot happened in a week, as I will tell you.

I realised that my feelings for Mike were not strong enough to make the huge move and to commit to a life together. The next day I rang him to tell him I had met someone else and that it was over. Of course, he was furious and accused me of having been seeing the new guy for months. He couldn't understand how I could end our relationship after meeting someone for one night. That was exactly the same as he had done with his seventeen-year relationship, though, wasn't it? He didn't speak to me for about a year and a half. After that he wrote and asked if we could still be friends, which we still are.

After the weekend, I drove to a local seaside town on the Monday to see an evening of clairvoyance at a hotel. It was a great night, and I set off to drive home still thinking about the night's happenings. When I reached the outskirts of my home town, the red light came on the dashboard of my car. It was midnight and raining. I didn't fancy the idea of stopping, and I was only seven miles from home. The car started to go slower and slower, and the lights started to dim. I could see my junction coming up and indicated to take the left turn so that I would be safely off the motorway. As I got onto the slipway, the car went bang and white smoke billowed out. As it came to a halt, I got out to take a look, not sure what I was looking for! A car slowed down. It was a couple who lived in my home town who knew me. They gave me a lift home, and I woke Jak who said we would take my other car and tow the broken one back home. We had only gone a short way when the car ran out of petrol. We walked home and drained petrol from his motorbike to fill the car that was empty, and then we towed my car home. By this time it was the early hours of the morning.

As soon as it was light, I went to Roger's garage and explained what had happened. He agreed to get it to his workshop and have a look at it. It was serious. I had made several holes in the pistons and cracked the head. We spent nearly all week together messing about with the car, finding second-hand parts, and generally getting to know each other. By the time Friday came round when we had arranged to go out on a date, we were already sure we wanted to be together. He moved in with me, and Jak moved into the flat that Roger had left, so it all worked out right and suited everyone. The car? Oh yes, it cost so much to repair that I couldn't afford it, so I had to marry him!! We tell people we didn't rush into a relationship. We moved in together after a week and got married a few months later. We have been together seventeen years now, and he is so very supportive of all I do. I couldn't do so much spiritual work without his support and his understanding that this work is my life's pathway.

Reiki Healing

R eiki was not something I had ever heard of. A man at church said he had just learnt how to be a channel for the reiki healing energy. He was so enthusiastic that I decided to find out more. He gave me the name and phone number of the lady he learnt with, and I decided to get in touch with her. She told me that reiki is an ancient Tibetan healing. She taught it in three levels and had a course in a month's time. I went along to the course. She was a lovely lady and told us all about this wonderful energy. It was the first time I had learnt anything to do with spiritual practises other than what I had been born with, and this set me off on a long learning journey. I finished the course, and she told us that if we wanted to do level two, she wanted us to wait at least six months and use the energy as much as we could. I was to contact her if I ever decided I wanted to go on further.

After six months I was eager to learn more, so I arranged to do level two with her. Again I found this wonderful energy so uplifting and was glad I had decided to do the course. She told us that we now had all the information we would need to work on ourselves, other people, animals, and plants. The only level left, she said, was master/teacher. If at any time any of us thought we would be running workshops and teaching it ourselves, she would need to be sure that we were ready to take the next step, and she would expect to see evidence of case studies. No way would I be doing that, I thought. My confidence and self-worth were still quite low, and I thought no one would be interested in listening to me.

One night my youngest son wanted to come to the spiritualist church with me. In the car Mom started telling us about her granny, who was a regular church goer. She said she would dress up in her Sunday best, put on a big black hat, and off she would go. She also said she had a wooden leg due to a childhood accident, but this didn't stop her doing anything she wanted to. The church service started and the medium made her link with the spirit world.

"I have a lady walking towards me," the clairvoyant said. "She is all in black and has a large black hat on. She has a slight limp. Oh no it's not a limp. She has a wooden leg."

Well, my son nearly choked after the conversation in the car and made a hasty retreat outside for a ciggie. She passed on the message that Mom's granny bought and then made a few other links. After a while she came back to me.

"You're very fond of animals, aren't you?" I said I was. "You had a pet chicken?" I nodded, remembering when the day the old chick was brought to me in a shoe box as it wasn't very well. He grew into a very handsome cockerel, and we called him Snudge. While I was day dreaming about the memory she added, "You used to dress it up and take it out in a doll's pram?" Everyone turned to look at me. I felt myself turning bright red as I nodded. "You have a wolf as your animal spirit guide. This usually means to me that you will be teaching spiritual work in the future." With this she finished her message and went on to someone else. Well she got that wrong, I thought. I could barely speak out in a shop when I want to be served, never mind teach anyone!

Not long after this we had a major change in our church. The chairman, secretary, and treasurer all upped sticks and moved within a few weeks. We had to quickly reform if we were to keep going. We also lost our venue, so we had to find other premises. I was asked if I would do the job as secretary. At first I said no due to my lack of confidence, but after being persuaded it would be easy and that I wouldn't have to speak out in front of people, I accepted. We carried on for a short while, and then the lady who ran the open circles decided she didn't want to do it any longer and asked if I would. Again I was too shy to accept. This shyness had stopped me doing such a lot in my life, and I heard myself say I would give it a try.

One day the phone rang. It was my reiki master. She told me she was leaving to go and work with the poor people in India, and if I ever thought I would like to do reiki master/teacher training with her, I had better decide within the next month. I really wanted to do this and asked my guides if I should take this next step. Of course, the answer wasn't yes or no; I should just follow my heart and trust that all would be well. If I was to follow my heart, I would definitely do it. One big snag though—I had no money to pay for it. Spirit said to follow my heart. If I really wanted this, I would find a way. Having a house and a mortgage, I was already doing three jobs to keep our heads above water. There simply weren't enough hours in a day to do any more work. So I decided to sell the last bits of jewellery I had and raised exactly the amount needed to do this course. I have never regretted this and thank spirit every day for giving me the support to believe in myself more.

The next ten years or more were very busy. By now I had met and married Roger, and life had settled down. He was very supportive of what I did with the spirit world. I was helping others and was learning many new therapies to add to my tool box. The teaching and circles started with one group of about seven people. This quickly grew, so I started a second circle to accommodate the numbers. Most days were taken up with dog walking, working on a switchboard in the mornings, and doing therapies and clairvoyance in the afternoons and evenings. The small donation I asked people for to sit in a circle was a good way of giving something back, and I supported numerous animal charities. At last I felt I was using whatever it was that I was given from spirit to help others.

One day my guides said they didn't want me to give any more clairvoyant messages to people. I couldn't believe I was hearing right. I had always done this, so I ignored it and carried on. The message was said to me many times, and every time I ignored it. I felt I was doing what I should be. One day I had a lady sitting in front of me who was desperate for a reading. She had lost her mother and was looking for evidence that life goes on after death. I explained to her that we can't ask people to come to us. They come to us on a love link and have freewill, so I wasn't sure that her mother would come through, but someone she knew would and hopefully it would be her mother. I asked my guides to help me, and there was silence. I asked again, and still there was silence. Panic set in. I had always had them there till now. I told the lady I would give her a reading psychically instead of clairvoyantly and asked if this would be okay. She nodded, and I finished the reading. After she left I asked again, "Where are you?" This time they spoke.

"We have suggested to you not to do any more readings for people. There is other work for you to do. You will always be able to see and hear us. Times and energies are changing fast. Sometimes people consult a medium to guide them through times of their life when they feel challenged. If you guide them through these troubles, they do not have the opportunity to learn from those troubles. So the troubles come back in another form, sometimes harder to learn than if they worked their way through them when they first arose. These are sometimes challenges they set for themselves before they came to earth. Times are changing more than you can possibly imagine. Everyone chose to be on earth at this exciting time. Use your time and energy to put their feet on their own unique spiritual pathway. If they are finding life hard, help guide them through it using another tool from your toolbox. Show them guidance and spiritual support. Help them link with their own spirit guides, and tell them of the importance of unconditional love."

Well, I can't say I was happy about this at first, but the word "trust" gets thrown about a lot, and I did trust. I didn't have to wait long. Even more people wanted to join a circle to learn more about their own spiritual lives, and I was busy with other therapies that encourage people to locate their own strength in whatever situation they find themselves.

Sometimes things unfold slowly and don't seem to make any sense at the time. One of these times was when I started seeing another chakra. I usually see them as a swirling mass of energy that opens and closes as we live our lives and get on with our business. They affect the aura and the colours the aura show. There seemed to be an extra energy centre between the throat and the heart and slightly to the left. It usually showed as a turquoise colour or sometimes just as a change in the energy around that area. I asked all of my spiritual friends, and no one seemed to have been aware of it. It was more prominent on men. As I couldn't find out what it meant, I asked my guides. They said it was a chakra that would help balance the male/female energies as we approached what we people on earth were calling a new age. So this was why it is more prominent in men as we are going into a feminine age. This would help balance the male/female energies in individuals. As time went by, this chakra seemed to be spoken about more and was mentioned in books. I also had a big increase in men wanting to join the circle and learn more about spiritual development. So now I listen and watch what is being shown to me. If it doesn't make sense, I file it away to be used when the time is right.

Travelling Tales

T ravelling has always been important. I love going to other countries and seeing their customs and how the people live. Maybe this is because I was encouraged by my parents from an early age to see that travelling widens the horizons of the mind. One day while I was in another country, I felt an overwhelming urge to send healing to the place I was in, not to the earth but to the energies of things that had occurred over the years. So I stood on a rock overlooking the sea and started channelling reiki. It felt right, so I stood for quite a while. I asked spirit what had happened in this place, and they told me that the area was well known for battles and torture. A lot of blood had been spilled using prisoners as human sacrifices. They said anyone could stand and send out thoughts of love and light to help cleanse areas that were holding onto this sort of energy. It would also help to stand on a ley line and send healing light through it. Ley lines get blocked by lots of things and can affect people who live on a blocked ley line. So I decided that when I went to places to visit, I would always spend some time sending out love and light and would encourage others to do the same.

Visiting very spiritual SEDONA

Riding a Texas Long Horn

My travels have been educational, relaxing, and humorous at times. Sometimes they have also been life-changing, as was the first visit to Spain in 1963. Travelling abroad was fairly new to me and my family. We loved the sunshine and meeting local people, seeing the different architecture and learning about the local customs. One man told us we should go to see a bullfight; it was exciting, and we could see the brave matadors in action. He could see we were a bit worried about it, but he assured us it wasn't cruel because sometimes the bull won! With his encouragement we went along. There were six fights, and after the first five minutes, I was sick and wanted to leave. There was no way out as it was packed, so I sat with my hands over my eyes and ears for the rest of the afternoon. I can't start to tell you about the cruelty. It's far too horrific. That evening the hotel served roast beef fresh from the bullring that afternoon. Again I was physically sick, and I told my parents I would never eat anything dead again. That was over fifty years ago, and I have never eaten meat or fish since that day. My friends laugh at me when I explain I don't eat anything that has ever had a face.

Visiting the death railway in Thailand, I was sending out love and light to the area, thinking how terrible it must have been to have to work in that heat and to be starving as well. We were told how the prisoners used to put their feet and hands that had sceptic sores into the river and let the fish nibble away at the infected areas. Later I went for a walk over the bridge. This was not the original bridge over the river Kwai, which I think was blown up, but a rebuilt version. It was a bit worn and had huge holes where we could clearly see the river below. We walked along and suddenly heard a train coming. I couldn't believe this was still a working bridge. We quickly leapt to the side to avoid the train and were careful not to fall into the river. That was one time I nearly needed to send healing to myself!

Back at the hotel we got talking to two ladies from the United Kingdom. One was interested in what I do and asked if I could pass on any message from her husband. I told her that if he did make contact with me while I was there, I would happily pass on the messages. After two weeks there was still no contact with him, but then, nearly at the end of the holiday, a man from the spirit world approached and said he was with the lady who wanted a message. He told me that he approved of her new kitchen and that she had done the right thing with her investments. Just before he went, he told me to tell her she was going to be a grandma. I passed on the message, and she took a picture from her bag to show me and asked if it was him. I was shocked. This man was not the spirit. What could have happened? Spirit had never let me down before, then she smiled and said, "I'm sorry to test you, but I had to be sure you were telling the truth. The picture is my brother, who is very much alive." Phew! Then she said she could accept all of what he told me but not the baby message, as neither of her daughters wanted children since they were career girls. Later on after I arrived home, I received an email from her to say her daughter had picked her up from the airport and announced she was pregnant.

That was a busy day in Thailand. Next, my dad came to me from the spirit world and said my cousin had died. She had a heart attack, and he wanted me to know she was safe on the other side with them.

Another time Roger and I were in Turkey on holiday. We decided it would be a good idea to take a twelve-hour coach trip to Istanbul as we would see some of the country. Once we had bought our tickets, we realised the coach set off at 10.00 p.m., so we would not see very much in the dark. The journey was slow, and after a couple of near misses on the roads, I decided I wasn't going to sleep but would stay awake and watch the road as I had no intention of joining my friends in spirit just yet. The driver said he was calling in to a bus station for a short break and a loo stop. When I got into the ladies', I soon realised that all the ladies getting ready in there were ladies of the night who were getting ready for their night's work. Suddenly one lady ran out of the loo with her skirt round her waist screaming, "Ahhhhhhhh! Rat! Rat! Rat!" There was a huge black rat running across the walls and doors causing panic. I followed the line of woman and ran outside— much to the amusement of the men outside.

After another couple of hours, we made another stop. I was still bemused from the rat encounter, but I needed the loo, so I made my way down the three flights of stairs to the ladies'. The gents' was on one level and the ladies' a bit lower down, so I told Roger to stop and wait for me by the door to the gents'. When I got to the ladies', there was a turnstile to get in with an attendant to operate it, but he was asleep. Not wanting to wake him, I climbed over the turnstile and closed the cubicle door. A few moments later while I was washing my hands, I felt a grip on my shoulder. The sleeping attendant had woken up. Terrified, I ran out, fell over the turnstile, and with tights ripped and knees bleeding, ran up the flights of stairs to Roger. When he saw the mess I was in and me blabbering about a man, he said, "What did he do?" By now I had got over the shock and was back to normal and in a very quiet voice I said he had offered me a piece of melon. We had to laugh about it, but at the time it wasn't so funny.

We were very hungry when we got to Istanbul, so we set off to find a meal—not too easy as my strict vegetarian diet seemed to be a problem everywhere. Everything we were offered was seafood, meat, or eggs. Suddenly Roger said, "Don't look!" This was the worst thing to say to me as I had to look. There was a large cabinet rotisserie going round with a dozen sheep's heads on it. Yuk! Not far further on we found a lovely traditional restaurant and had garlic bread and lentils.

Later on that day we shared a taxi with a mother and daughter. I couldn't stop looking at her. I have never seen so many people from the spirit world around a single person. She looked sad and haunted. We got talking, and she told me she was researching her family history. Without thinking, I blurted out, "Well you have certainly got plenty on the other side of life to help you."

She sat upright. "Why? What can you tell me?" I mentioned a few of the people who were with her, and said that they all wanted to speak at once. She confirmed that she knew these people and that she was the only survivor. She was Jewish, and her family had all been killed in the War.

When I was seeing Mike from Canada, we sometimes stayed at a particular hotel in Jamaica. The owner got to know us quite well, and one day he asked me to go into his office as he had a problem. A guest had died in one of the rooms a short while earlier, and the cleaners were afraid to go in as they had heard moaning and groaning, as he put it. I said I would have a look, and if there was a spirit there I would help it to the other side. I went into the room, followed by the manager carrying a large crucifix. I laughed and asked if he was planning to knock the spirit on the head with it. Much to his relief, there was nothing to do. Some of the guests had been playing tricks on the cleaners after hearing they were superstitious. To thank us the manager took us out to a local restaurant he liked. I noticed a chicken running around that had no feathers at all. It looked strange, and I laughed, only to be told off by the owner who told me it was a spirit chicken.

"No," I said, "it's alive."

"No, it's a spirit chicken." Then I realised that he meant it was a spiritual chicken. He said that if anyone cast a hex on him and buried a mojo bag in his garden, the chicken would scratch it out and break the spell. You learn something every day!

There were several stray dogs around the hotel, and I used to feed them. They used to sleep by our door in the shade. One day I heard some local lads shouting, so I went to see what was happening. They were throwing one of the dogs that I used to feed off the high cliff into the sea below. Each time she would shake herself off and trot back to the top of the cliff and settle by our door. When I asked what they thought they were doing, they said, "She likes it. She has fleas. It's good for her."

The poor dog was panting and obviously didn't enjoy their game. I told them that if they threw her off again, they would follow soon after. They took me at my word and disappeared. The dog went back to sleep by our door. The next time we stayed at the hotel, one of the lads said, "I know you! You're that dog lady."

"Is she still about?"

"Yes, we at the hotel have sort of taken to looking after her." So that was a good ending for the dog. Later I saw her, and she did look quite well looked after.

Another night I heard gun shots, three of them. The next day I asked if anyone had heard the shots. No one had except one man. He was a policeman from Miami. He said, "I sure did. I know the sound of gunfire."

Later that night I saw the hotel guard and asked, "Did you hear gun shots last night?"

"Yes, it was me. I shot at an intruder."

"There were three shots."

"Yes, I missed him twice.

The first time I ever went to Jamaica was with a girlfriend. We both wanted some sunshine and a few weeks without any worries, and we thought it would be the perfect place to take a holiday. On the first day we decided to take a walk to the local beach. It was fairly busy, so we found a quiet spot and lay in the sun. Soon we were disturbed by a gang of about six men. They started messing about with our handbags, throwing them to each other. One sat down and wrapped his legs around my friend as she sat on the sand and tried to kiss her while his friend took photographs with her camera. She screamed and shouted to me to do something. Just then two men came running up the beach with baseball bats and chased them off. They told us we shouldn't be there alone. We were really grateful for their help and bought them cans of Pepsi to say thank you. They said that if we wanted to see any of the sights they would be happy to be our bodyguards. The rest of the holiday went well, and we saw places that only the locals go to. We really had a lot of fun, and most important of all, we were safe.

One day I wanted to go up into the mountains. My friend wasn't well and stayed at the hotel. I hired a motorbike and took my Jamaican bodyguard as a passenger. Soon we were miles away from the town and really enjoying the scenery. It was getting late, and I thought we should be heading back. He said he had friends close by and we could go and see them before heading back. We found the house. It had been partly destroyed by Hurricane Gilbert years before. I noticed the bike was nearly out of fuel, and it was getting dark. The fireflies were darting about, and I was really concerned at the predicament I found myself in. There didn't seem to be any women about, but there were about twelve men. They were polite, but I was uneasy. My bodyguard assured me they were fine and had said I could stay the night as it was dark and there was no fuel to be found anywhere locally. It would be safer to stay until it got light. I felt this was a time I really needed the advice of my spirit guides. They told me all was well and not to be afraid. I remembered I had a bottle of brandy in a bag with the motorbike, which had been carried up the steps and into the house. When I got back they were all smoking huge spliffs and offered me one. I declined and offered them brandy. They declined and said they didn't drink. Slowly we all chilled out, and some of them decided they would try a brandy. Not being used to alcohol, they were soon quite drunk. Then I realised everyone was disappearing. The owner of the house said that there was only one bed and I could use it. The others slept in the garden. The room was sparse, to say the least—a wardrobe with no doors, propped up on bricks, and with one change of clothes hanging in there, no glass in the windows, no floor covering, and a bed covered in only a very old nylon sheet. I lay there listening to the jungle sounds for a long time, and when I was sure everyone had gone to sleep, I managed to sleep a bit as well. My dreams were all over the place, and I was relieved to wake and see my guides close by.

Soon it was morning, and slowly people came from in the garden to the house, where they made me hot tea and showed me where a stream ran through the property so I could have a wash. I asked where the toilet was, and they pointed to a wooden hut at the bottom of the garden. They told me not to sit on the seat but to stand on it and then crouch down. I made my way to the "toilet" and realised it only had a small half door. I was worried that they might see me in the loo, so I decided it was easier to go into the woods. As I stepped down from the seat, there was a loud crash, and I fell straight through the rotten floor, hanging by my arms. I was frantic to pull my shorts up as the men came running to see what had happened. It was only when they dragged me out that I felt that my arm was hurting badly. I had cut it on the sharp wood, and it was bleeding. One of the men grabbed a handful of green leaves and started rubbing it on the arm. When I complained and told him to stop, he said, "It's just herb. It will stop the pain."

Eventually we pushed the bike a couple of miles to another house, where the owner sold us enough fuel to get to a filling station. As we rode back towards the town, we were stopped by the police. The bike didn't have the right tax disc to travel out of the town's boundaries, they said. They asked for my passport, looked at it, and told me to go. My friend didn't have any ID, so he was told he would have to appear in court the next week. I was really upset, as he was told he would go to prison if he couldn't pay the fine. I was going home before the case was heard. He phoned me and said he had been fined £25, so I sent it over to him via a company that sends money abroad. It was only when we were on the way back to the hotel that I realised I had stayed the night at a ganja farm, and I smelt like it too!

Later on that day my friend and I decided to go rafting on the river. The rafts were made of bamboo and were guided along the river by a raft captain who used a long pole to push the raft through the water. It was very hot, and we had on our shorts. My friend was wearing a swimsuit with a padded top that increased her bust by three sizes. It looked very impressive with the shirt over it, and we were both laughing at her sudden increase in size. The raft captain was impressed as well and couldn't take his eyes of her. He kept saying, "It's so hot. Are you girls hot?" We said that we were, and he was encouraging her to take off her shirt. Eventually she took off her shirt, being careful to lean back so as not to give the secret away. He was watching her so intently that he hit a high spot in the river. The raft overturned, throwing us all into the water. As we scrambled to get to the shore, I noticed that he had cut his leg badly. I asked him if I could give him some reiki. He agreed, and the look of disappointment on his face was priceless as he noticed my friend looked completely different now that she was sitting up bandaging his cut leg with her handkerchief.

One of the things I like to do is take holiday cruises. I like nothing better than to be on a ship in the middle of nowhere with the moon shining down and watch the ocean. It's here that I feel as close to spirit as anywhere. I was on board a ship once, and the next day was midsummer solstice. Knowing I would be up and about to see the sunrise very early, I thought I would warn the captain that if he saw me on deck looking suspicious at sunrise, I wasn't going to throw myself overboard but was just worshiping the sun god. He looked surprised and said "Bloody hell!" I was worried that I might have upset him, but he said, "The solstice? If it's the solstice tomorrow, then it's also my wedding anniversary, and I haven't got a card for my wife." With this he disappeared, probably wondering how he could get a card in the middle of the ocean. The next day as the sun came up I started my ritual at the front of the ship. I cast my circle and started drawing up earth energy through my feet, and I felt all wobbly and fell over. Then I realised I was on water, so there wasn't any earth energy to draw up. Silly witch!

A few memories come to mind. Once I was getting a cup of tea from a tea and coffee station on board another ship when I was aware of the spirit of a man. He told me his wife was sitting close by, and would I tell her he was all right? I shook my head and told him it was a bit awkward to approach a stranger with that information. He said, "Please tell her. Look how sad she is." Reluctantly I sat by the lady and struck up a conversation. Was she enjoying the holiday? Did she like the ship? She shook her head and said her husband had recently died, and she had been going to cancel the holiday as it was supposed to be for both of them. At the last moment she decided to go alone and was now regretting it. She said she had realised it was a mistake, and she had spent all day thinking about him and wondering where he was, as she believed in an afterlife. I steered the conversation around to evidence of survival to see what her thoughts were of an afterlife. I didn't want to offend her if she had strong different beliefs. Eventually I was able to convey the husband's message that he was all right and never far away from her.

She looked at me and said, "Do you know where he is now?"

Without thinking, I said, "Yes, he is by the coffee machine." Then I realised how stupid that sounded, before making a hasty retreat.

On one ship we were ready to disembark and were sitting around a table with several other people waiting for the announcement that we could leave the ship. Suddenly a man appeared from spirit and said, "That's my son sitting opposite to you. He is an artist and has given it all up since I passed over. He is really struggling, and I have to get a message to him to tell him I am so sorry that I was never able to show him any affection or ever say how good his paintings were. The real reason was that I was envious of him because he was so talented, and I ignored him and never praised his work. Now I want to say I am sorry. Tell him I love him and that when I was alive on earth I couldn't show it. Tell him that I want him to paint again. His hands have seized up with the anger and frustration I left him with. If he starts to paint, his hands will free up."

Well how was I going to open up that conversation? When the son started to rub his hands as if he was in pain, I asked him, "Are you all right?"

"No, my hands are all crampy, and it's getting me down."

I asked if he wanted me to give him some healing. He shook his head and then asked me why I wanted to help him. I just said that maybe it might help. He was sure he didn't need or want any help, but he stayed polite. Just then Roger decided to visit the loo, and the man also went. Roger later told me that the man had asked him what I did and how I could help. Roger told him I was a medium and that he should ask me if I had a message for him.

When they came back, he said, "I have to get off the ship soon, and your husband said you might have a message for me?"

I was able to pass on his dad's message. He said he would go home and start painting again, as he always thought he didn't live up to his dad's expectations. Spirits usually find a way to get their message to us in one way or another.

While visiting a small Caribbean island, we decided to have a walk around the local market. It was hot, and I had on a summer strappy vest and shorts and wore one of my top hats covered in cockerel feathers as it was hot and I don't like ordinary sun hats. We walked around all day and bought quite a few trinkets. Several people remarked on the tattoo on my shoulder, which is a witch riding a broomstick. There were comments of "Magician? Sorcerer?" I just smiled and said nothing, as I wasn't sure of the local customs and beliefs. This was lucky. When we got back to the ship, I read in the ship's newsletter that witchcraft is illegal in this particular place and is punishable by prison.

On another ship I was with my mom. We were having a cup of tea, and I said, "I have a lady here from spirit. She wants me to give her granddaughter a message." Between us we decided it wasn't a good idea, even though I was told the granddaughter was sitting right behind me. So I was adamant, I said no.

The next day the spirit lady was back, and she told me her name was Philamena and added, "My granddaughter is at the next table to you. Please give her a message. Just say you have spoken to me and that she has made the right decision and not to change her mind."

So I approached the group of youngsters and said, "You're going to think I am off my trolley, but . . . ," and passed on the message. The girl in question ran away crying. Sod it, I thought. I knew I shouldn't have said anything. Now I would probably be thrown off the ship or worse if she reported me as a nutter. Later that day I had to go to book an excursion and was surprised to see the girl there. She worked for the ship! She asked me how I got the message.

"How did you speak to her?" As I was starting to explain it, she stopped me. "I mean, how did you communicate? She was Sicilian and couldn't speak any English."

I suppose language is no barrier if we are communicating with our mind and not with words. She then said she had made a huge decision and had been thinking of changing her mind till her gran intervened.

For quite a while my guides had been asking me to visit Poland and go to the Auschwitz concentration camp. I was willing and asked Roger if he would come with me. He said he wouldn't really want to as he thought it would be a bit heavy. I was happy to go on my own, but I thought it would be better to have a friend to go with. A man from church said he would go, and he would look for a cheap air fare. One came up, and it was booked that we would go in March. When I told my friend Addy, who is also a hereditary witch like me, she said she would go as well if her husband would look after their son. So the three of us went together and booked a hotel in Krakow. My guides had told me not to get drawn into the things we saw and heard. Instead I should try to do what I always did and spread love, light, and healing to the area. As you can imagine, it's very easy to get drawn into the sadness of the things that happened. Addy was four months pregnant at the time, and I was a bit worried about her, but she managed fine.

*Inside Auschwitz concentration camp, the square
shows the spirit picture.*

The visit wasn't at all what we imagined. We were
aware of all the things we were hearing about on our
headphones. The area felt devoid of energy, and I
was surprised we didn't see any spirits even in the gas
chambers or the crematorium areas. It was as if when
people were sent there, they had given up. Looking at the
pictures all over the walls, their eyes all looked soulless.
Addy and I decided to connect to some of the large trees
that were on the grounds, which would probably have
been there for a number of years. Again they were not
saying anything. It is unusual not to pick up energy from
a tree.

I was so pleased that we all went together, as I think
three of us all trying to send out love, light, and healing
was much better than if I had gone on my own. When we
got home, I was intrigued by some of the photographs we

had taken. One shows a small figure in one of the sheds where around 200 people were kept. It looks about the size of a child. I really didn't see any spirit while I was there. Another one shows a dark shape in the sky. When it's enlarged, it looks like a black angel shape. When I sent it to a friend who lives in Poland, she said that Krakow is protected by the energy of the dark queen, who some say has been seen in the skies and is depicted with wings.

I have so many travel stories! A few stand out in my memory, and this is one of them. On a recent journey to the United States we were going through immigration. My documents were checked and my fingerprints taken as usual. The customs man looked at my pentagram necklace and ring and asked, "Are you a sorcerer? What is your reason for visiting the USA?"

I couldn't resist teasing him by telling him I was on my way to New Orleans to get some voodoo supplies. We usually travel light, so we only had hand luggage with us. We placed our cases on the area to go through the X-ray. Roger's went straight through, but I looked at the screen, and there was a most peculiar shape showing in my case. It looked like a hair dryer, which obviously resembled a gun! I knew I had nothing in the case of that shape. They sent it through again, and there it was again. The officer called his manager, who asked me to open my bag, which I did. There was nothing in it that resembled the shape, so he zipped it up and sent it back through the X-ray, and there it was again! The boss picked up my case, came over to me, looked at my brooch of Merlin, and asked if he was looking at Merlin. I told him he was. He waved his hand, smiled, and said, "Off you go then." I'm not sure what the spirit world was up to that day, but luckily the boss man had a sense of humour.

Recently while we were travelling in the States, I realised we were very close to Wounded Knee, where one of my spirit guide's body is buried from his last incarnation on earth. I asked if we could visit the grave to take a picture, and Roger agreed to take me there. I was so disappointed to get there and see how overgrown it was. I was too worried about snakes to continue. Roger knew how important it was to me and took my camera to get me my photograph. It was quite surreal to see the grave with my guide's name on it while also seeing him standing beside me and hearing him speak to me as usual.

And finally from travel tales . . .

My dad had a mentally disabled brother whom he used to take out for a car ride every Monday morning. When he died, I went with Dad to collect his ashes. As Dad put the urn on the front seat of the car, he said, "I am taking you for your last car ride," and patted the urn playfully. Suddenly a car pulled out in front of us, and we had to brake hard, sending the urn flying off the seat and spilling the ashes. When we got home we didn't know what to do, so we decided to get the ash up with the vacuum cleaner and then empty the lot back into the urn to scatter. Knowing that Mom wouldn't approve of being in a car with human ashes in it, we never told her, but she picked up on the sideways glances between us every time she sat in the front seat of the car!

My Dogs

Dogs have always been a huge part of my life. As I said earlier, I didn't walk or talk till I was two, but I did bark. Mom says I could copy any noise a dog made and any type of bark. I would bark to any dogs I saw in the street, and they would answer and then follow us with Mom pushing me in the pushchair and saying, "Please don't call them, Lyn."

Lyn doing a firewalk for WAG (dog group)

One day I saw an old fox-fur stole belonging to an aunt of mine. Feeling the fur and hugging it close, it reminded me of something. I'm not sure, but it was almost like a distant memory. The fur felt comforting, and the fox fur (known affectionately as "Foxy") became a constant companion. It went everywhere with me, and over the years it became almost threadbare. At that age I had no knowledge of the cruelty connected with killing animals for their fur. All I knew was that I liked the feel of it.

Cooling off in a bucket of ice water, notice the many spirit orbs around myself and Addy

As a family we had several dogs, all with their different personalities and habits. I couldn't imagine life without having a dog. In later years I think that looking after dogs has been a balance to my spiritual life. While some people might think I spend a lot of time away with the faeries, looking after a dog provides a great balance. No one can feel spiritual when walking barefoot on the grass and treading on a squishy dog turd, can they? The only time I didn't have a dog of my own was when I was with David. I knew that any aggression he had towards me he would take out on my dog. Not wanting to risk this, I used to spend time with a friend's dogs and made do with that.

Lyn and her dogs

As soon as I was beginning to feel settled with Jamie, I got a German Shepherd pup that I called Ben. He was one of those once-in-a-lifetime dogs, a perfect temperament, no trouble at all. We were not only telepathic but inseparable as well. I decided to join a local dog-training class and really enjoyed this contrast to my spiritual life. The opportunity came along to train as a dog-training instructor. The course was at a veterinary college and was a week's residential. We all took along our dogs to use them to learn with. From day one everyone was finding the course hard because the training and methods seemed very harsh. The instructors stripped us of any self-confidence and made fun of everything we did. With my confidence at zero, I spent most nights crying into Ben's fur, telling him all my secrets and worries, and ending with "I didn't want to come on this bloody course in the first place." He listened patiently for me to stop ranting and then licked my face and nuzzled me to get me to smile. The days were long and hard. Looking back at it, I realise that their methods were intended to ensure that we had the confidence to stand up in front of a class and actually instruct. We had to be able to sort out any problems. It didn't seem like this at the time, and several of us went home after being laughed at or ridiculed by the instructors once too often.

A witches naming day for Addy's baby, Sidney

Ben and I stuck it out, though. One day we were being shown various ways to put a dog into the down position and then get it from the down to a stand. Ben and I were the ones chosen to practise on. One lady was bought forward to instruct me and Ben.

"Stand astride the dog," she said. I was trying hard to shake my head, as I am quite short and Ben was a very big GSD. "Yes, do as I say," she said in her best dog trainer's voice, trying to sound confident. So following her orders, I put Ben into the down position. When we came to put him in the standing position with me straddling his back, you can imagine what happened. I did a somersault over his back and ended up in a heap.

"What went wrong?" bellowed the instructor.

"She's too short," the lady said.

"Ha ha! Shall we put her on the rack and stretch her?"

"The dog's too tall."

"Ha ha! Shall we cut his legs off?"

The poor lady ran off in tears, and I couldn't help feeling sorry for her.

The week passed, and I was so pleased to pass the course. I was now a member of the British Institute of Professional Dog Trainers. This was a huge boost to my confidence. I wasn't useless, as David had told me all those years ago when he was robbing me of any confidence. I had achieved this and could achieve other things if I set my mind to it. When I returned home, I volunteered to join an organisation that helps abused women and also several other organisations that helped people in various ways. Now that I had more confidence, I trained in pet psychology and complementary therapies for animals.

When Ben was three, I bought another GSD, a bitch which I called Haley as she was born on the day Haley's comet was visible in the United Kingdom in the 1980s. She was so different to Ben, feisty and bad-tempered, an absolutely guard dog through and through. She got me into so many scrapes over the years. I needed all the dog-training qualifications I had worked so hard to get. One thing in particular I remember was when she was a puppy. In a single week she ate the back of the washing machine and flooded the kitchen, ate all the moulding from the inside of the fridge leaving just the insulation showing, chewed her way through a solid door, and ate all the plants in the house. She wasn't a popular dog at all! When I came home from work one day and saw she had clawed strips from the wallpaper under the window, I decided to put it back together to get her out of trouble. Painstakingly I fitted each piece back on the wall. It was like a jigsaw puzzle and took several hours. When Jamie came in from work, he looked straight at it and asked what had happened. Glancing quickly at my handiwork, I thought, "How could he possibly know? I have done a good job." Then he told me he had taken off the paper before going to work to see how easy it would come off when he started decorating. I should have realised honesty is the best policy!!

Haley calmed down, and when she was four I introduced her to a GSD stud dog. He had an excellent pedigree and temperament. Eventually she gave birth to several puppies and didn't seem to be having any trouble at first. But then she seemed to struggle. I rang the vet who told me that a puppy might be stuck and asked if I could feel any legs. I did, and I helped her to give birth to a huge male pup that turned out to be fine. He was quickly followed by another male that must have been too long in the birth canal as he was not breathing. I quickly cleared him from the birth sac, cleared his mouth, and massaged him with a towel. I breathed into his tiny mouth and then put a drop of brandy on his tongue. He coughed and spluttered and appeared all right. Altogether Haley had seven pups. When I got up the next day, one was dead. I was so sad, as I thought it was the pup I had helped, but it wasn't; the tiny dead puppy was a bitch.

I knew at that point that I would never be able to part with the puppy I had helped, so he joined my growing pack as dog number three, and I called him Edmund. He had inherited his mother's feisty temper, but I was determined to work hard with him and train him well. When he was about ten months old, I was walking over the local moors on November 6. The previous night, being bonfire night, had seen loads of fireworks. With their whizz-bangs and bright flashes, they are not at all enjoyable for animals. Suddenly a large stallion ran out towards us. He lived on the moors and may have been still spooked by the previous night's fireworks. He reared up and came down with a heavy thud of the hoof on Edmund's head. The poor dog dropped like a stone. He had blood coming out of his nose and mouth and seemed to be dead. I ran over to him and was surprised to see him open his eyes, shake his head, and get up. He had the hoof print on his head for a week! After that he was a different dog. He didn't like visitors to the house or other dogs, and he didn't seem very bright at all. My dog-training friends used to say that the lights were on but no one was home. We had him for another fourteen years, and we loved him dearly. Roger used to say he would trust him with his life, but he wouldn't trust him with yours!

Next came Myrlyn. I knew the breeder where he came from. A friend of mine had bought a puppy from him, but after a week my friend's wife decided dogs made too much mess, and he was returned to the breeder. I was so sorry that this poor pup had been returned that I offered to buy him to join our merry pack. For a year he was known as "Overdraft"!

Roger loved all the dogs as I did, but he said he would like us to buy one together and raise it from a puppy. We gained another GSD and called her Morgan. She was a very small dog compared to the others, but she soon became pack leader, and a very good pack leader she was too! Our house was rather crowded, and about this time we moved to another place. It was much bigger, so when Roger came home and said he knew of a litter of GSDs looking for homes, we decided to get another. This was Gwynnavere. She seemed to have problems from day one. From an early age she had an itchy skin. The vets couldn't seem to help her, and we tried loads of alternative remedies and regularly took her to the sea for a swim, which seemed to be the only thing that helped her.

One New Year's Day I came down stairs and noticed my beloved Ben was lying in a pool of his own pee. He was losing the feeling in his rear end as GSDs often do, and as I helped him to stand to clean him up, I realised that he was also covered in poo. I cleaned him up and made him comfortable. As I looked into those beautiful brown eyes, I sensed him say, "Please help me. I am so tired and want to go home." Just thinking about this still brings tears to my eyes even after all these years. I rang the vet who arranged to come to the house later that day. Then I cooked a pound of liver for Ben, which he loved, and gave him some chocolate, which is not good for dogs but he liked it. The vet arrived and agreed there was nothing anyone could do and the kindest thing was to let him go.

I said my goodbyes and held him till his soul left his body. We lit a candle for him, and the vet stayed with us until I was ready to let him be taken away. I cried for hours and hours and felt my heart chakra close down with the grief.

One of my guides, who always leads a white horse, stepped forward. He tells me we have had many lifetimes together, the most recent during the crusades. I don't remember this life we had together, but I have known the guide as long as I can remember in this life. He said, "When the dog's ready, he can walk with me and the horse."

"His name is Ben," I said. There was silence from my guide as he waited for me to compose myself.

"He can walk with me and the horse," he repeated. After a short while I started seeing Ben with my guide and his horse. It's the nearest to actually having him still here with me on earth, and I thank spirit every day for this.

We lost Haley at the age of sixteen and Edmund at fifteen. As I sat with Edmund while the vet put him to sleep I whispered to him that I had been there when he was born into this world and would be there when he left this world. I told him I loved him so much and asked him to come back and see me soon. The next day I took a picture of the dogs playing, and there was a distinct shadow of another GSD. Maybe this was Edmund? I like to think so.

After Morgan we had Pendragon, another bitch. The vet said, "Pendragon was a man, wasn't he?" So she became known as Lady Pendragon.

Poor Gwynavere got worse and slowly lost every bit of fur. We used to shower her every day, smooth her all over with moisturising cream, and then put an old tee shirt on her to protect her skin. She had every test we could think of, but we never found anything to help her. One day she fell off the chair and seemed to have had a very short fit. After this her health got worse even though she was only seven. The vet said she had suffered a stroke. Soon she had another stroke which paralysed her, and we had to have her put to sleep on Valentine's Day.

Myrlyn developed a bad back leg and was diagnosed with a tumour. It was cancer. We were told that it might stay in the leg or it might spread. His leg got swollen and heavy, but he still had a good quality of life. We made him little shoes to wear on his bad foot so that it wouldn't rub on the ground and become sore. One night I gave him his food, and he threw it all back up. The same thing happened the next day. I was due to go on a short cruise the following day with Mom, as it was my birthday and she was treating me as a birthday gift. Before I left I made an urgent appointment at the vet's to see if he could prescribe some medication to help him. He said it was very serious. The cancer had spread to Myrlyn's stomach, and he wasn't going to get any better, being unable to keep any food or water down. He said he would suffer if I waited till I got back from the cruise. Not ever wanting that, I had to make the terrible decision to have him put to sleep. What a birthday!

With all the worry about Myrlyn, I hadn't even packed a case. The taxi was due in an hour. A holiday was the last thing on my mind, but Mom was looking forward to it, so through the tears I threw some clothes into a case and set off. When we reached the ship, I said to Mom. "I haven't a clue what I packed!" I opened the case and took out six coats and underwear, so I had to wear the same top and trousers every day, dressed up with a different coat.

When I got back home, Roger said that Morgan hadn't been well. We wondered if she was missing Myrlyn, but when I looked closely at her I thought she looked a bit bloated. Back to the vet's, and this time my heart was in my mouth as he examined her. He took a sample of fluid, and it came out blood-stained from her tummy area. He said he was going to operate to see what was going on. We waited in the waiting room. I said to spirit, "Please let Morgan be all right. I don't ask for anything for myself usually, but I can't stand to lose another dog so quickly."

The vet came out, and it was bad news. She had a tumour on her liver. It had attached to her other organs, and blood was pumping into her tummy every time her heart beat. He led us into the operating room to say our goodbyes. This was not happening surely? Seeing her lying there looking fit and healthy, I couldn't believe she was about to die. While she was still under the anaesthetic the vet allowed her to slip away. All the other dogs had been close to me for several hours after their souls left their bodies, but as soon as Morgan's soul was free, I saw her bounding into the distance with only one look back. I hope she was running to be with the others. I felt angry and told the spirit world I felt let down. I told them I didn't want to speak to them and spent the rest of the day and night in total silence, ignoring all attempts to speak to me. The next day my North American Indian guide spoke. All he said was, "The dog was ready to come home."

Soon I realised that all the asking and praying wouldn't do any good if it was time for Morgan to go home. I knew that, but grief had clouded my thoughts. My guides had reminded me and shown me they were always there for me no matter what I go through, and I thank spirit every day for this.

So Pendragon was our only dog for three months. She was lonely, so eventually we decided it was time to look for another puppy. We looked at newspapers, rang breeders, asked friends, and checked the internet. It seemed there were no GSD puppies around. That night I was contacted in sleep by my sister Margaret, who had passed to the spirit world. She was holding a small fluffy black bundle of puppy, and she said, "Here's your dog."

"He is lovely Margaret," I replied, "but where is he?"

"He will find you tomorrow," she said with a smile.

When I woke up, the words were still very much in my mind. I switched on the computer even before I had got dressed. There was a message which said, "I understand you are looking for a GSD puppy? My sister's dogs have had twelve. Here they are." I saw the picture. There was the black fluffy bundle my sister had given to me on the astral the night before. Ringing the number and getting dressed at the same time, I called out to Roger to get dressed quickly.

"We are going up country," I said. "Our new dog's there."

When we arrived at the house, we were shown into the kitchen where the pups were with their mom and dad. The lady said she would put the adult dogs outside so we could have a good look. Then I saw him. He was looking at me. He sat quietly at the back not trying to push in or make a fuss. After I had him in my arms, I put my pendulum over him to dowse he was the right one. It gave a huge yes. This was my new dog. When the owners came in, I had Merlin and was ready to go. I think they were a bit shocked; most people want to ask questions or play with the puppies. Soon we were on the way home to meet Pendragon. Merlin fit in well. He seemed to be a mixture of all the dogs we had recently lost. So we had two dogs again, and we were all happy.

A few years later we were due to go on holiday. It was cancelled due to the volcanic ash cloud caused by a volcano erupting in Iceland that led to a complete stoppage of all air travel for a week. The airline gave us a refund, so we decided to get another dog. That year I had been to Cruft's with Addy, and she had to drag me away from the Leonbergers, so we decided to add a Leo to our doggie family. We had never had any other breed except German Shepherds for over forty years, and she was certainly different. The first night I had to phone the breeder, as I was so worried about her lack of puppy behaviour. She just lay there sleeping. The breeder said, "Oh, my dear, Leos don't move unless they have to." This took a bit of getting used to. She is a sweet gentle giant, and I am so pleased we decided to have Morgana La Fey to join us.

In the last few years dogs have had a lot of bad press. Usually it's about irresponsible dog owners not cleaning up after their dogs. After yet another article calling for a dog ban on green areas in our town, I decided to try to get some responsible dog owners together to see what we could do. I started a group which we called WAG. We try to promote responsible dog ownership in our town, put on dog shows, give talks to schools, and clear up our local parks and open spaces of dog poo to try to shame irresponsible owners. To raise funds Addy and myself decided to do a fire walk and a walk on broken glass. The sponsorship we received formed the base for our group's funding. We are ably assisted by several friends who also come to my development groups. We work closely with the local council to try to help with any dog-related problems.

Stranger Than Fiction

So many things have happened, and indeed I expect they may seem odd to some people. It's hard to remember a lot of them, but some stick in my mind. One of those times was when I was working three jobs to keep a roof above our heads. I had a cleaning job at 5.00 a.m., walked the dogs at 7.00 am, worked at my office job for five hours, and then walked the dogs again before doing my evening job from 6 p.m. until 10 p.m.

I was walking in the woods not too far from where I lived with my three GSDs, Ben, Haley, and Edmund. I saw an elderly man coming towards me and put the dogs on the leads. When he got closer, he smiled and said, "I have seen you about."

"Yes, I come here a lot."

"I know." He reached out to touch the dogs.

I pulled back, saying, "Don't touch these two. They are not very friendly." He smiled and ran his hand across Haley's back.

"No worry. They are all right."

We walked together for a short while, and he told me he had been to see to his bees over the other side of the hill. We chatted about the weather and the local landscape. We were nearly back at the car now, so I opened the hatchback as we stood side by side and allowed the dogs to jump in. Closing the lid, I turned to say goodbye, but he was nowhere to be seen. As he was somewhat elderly and slow, I couldn't believe he had gone anywhere so quickly. I ran to the left and the right, but there was still no sign of him, so I drove home. The next day at work I mentioned to a lady who lived near the woods about the meeting. She smiled and said, "Oh, that would be old Mr Northover (name changed). "He has been dead fifty years. He kept bees all of his life."

The office I worked in was an old manor house. It was a lovely house, and I had seen many spirits there from time to time. Several of my bosses had seen things also and told me of what they had seen when working late, but because they thought people would think them silly, they asked me never to mention who they were. One day I needed the loo, but I wasn't supposed to leave reception unattended. The switchboard was quiet, so I decided to nip to the loo and be back before I was missed. I was standing washing my hands and checking my hair in the mirror as we ladies do, when I saw the spirit of a lady coming up behind me. She was dressed in a black dress and a white apron and was carrying a huge tureen of (I suppose) soup. I watched in the mirror as she came nearer. She was totally unaware of me, and I held my breath as she passed straight through me and disappeared. What a shock! This had never happened before, and I didn't like it. I ran out of the loo and stood cowering outside to get my breath back. Then, realising how stupid the situation was, I crept back inside and nervously looked around before hurrying back to my switchboard.

I am often asked to go to people's houses, as they are sure they have a spirit presence. They want me to get rid of the spirit so they can live in peace. I never know what I will find when I go to these places, and I always go with an open mind. Most turn out not to be spirits. Strange noises are sometimes just water pipes or normal house creaks. People scare themselves and are convinced it's a ghost. Some are as simple as a blocked ley line, but some are genuine cases. There are quite a few different sorts of energies, in my opinion (which may not be correct). Sometimes I find it's a loved one trying to let their family know they are around. This is easy to deal with, as it's usually straightforward to speak directly to the spirit and pass on the message for them. Sometimes negative energy may have been brought to the house by people messing around with Ouija boards or doing a spell without really understanding what they are doing. This can open up gateways for negative energy or entities to come into our dimension. If this is the case, I would have to find out what they had been doing and try to put it right. This can be done by clearing the energy left behind by the person dabbling and by closing the gateway between dimensions. Sometimes it's nothing to do with the house or building but the actual ground the place it is built on. For that I will need the help of my guides to send healing back to the time of whatever happened and communicate with any spirits from that time. There can be several time lines involved.

A person may open up a channel to the lower energies by excessive drug taking or drinking and be totally unaware of what they are doing. I don't mean having a couple of drinks but getting rolling drunk night after night so that they are not in control of themselves at all.

What I call a haunting can happen if a person goes over to the other side quickly or tragically. They may not be aware that they have passed over. Again, I would link with the spirit world and ask that someone from the spirit world comes and takes them over. Most go quite willingly when they realise that there are people they know waiting to help them. Some spirits hang around, not wanting to go to the other side either because they are tied to the earth by greed and do not want to leave their possessions or because they may still want to experience earthly pleasures. There are other reasons, but these are the ones I usually find.

Then there is, of course, poltergeist activity. This can start with a few simple things like doors banging, taps turning on and off, or the TV changing channels on its own, but it can escalate to driving the people who live there out of their homes. This type of energy seems to affect water and electricity. I have found it's often linked to a person in the house around the age of puberty or someone who is having a very passionate love affair. It can be really bad, but it can stop just as quickly as it starts. One theory is that this type of energy is generated from the humans themselves by the high energy being experienced in their everyday life.

I was called to a house that was having all types of problems. It started off with the TV switching channels, light bulbs exploding, and wardrobe doors opening and banging on their own. The family was getting really scared. I went along with a friend, and we looked everywhere and asked a lot of questions to see if we could sort it out. I didn't see any spirits and couldn't feel any problem with the house or the land. While I was outside my friend said he saw a little girl of about eight or nine. She told him her name was Lucy, and she had a pain in her head. She was waiting for her father. When asked where her mother was, she replied that she hadn't seen her for a long time. By the time I got back inside, she had gone and wouldn't show herself to me at all. We decided to ask spirit to take her to the other side. We stood and sent out healing to her, and in our mind we created a pillar of light. We asked her to go and stand in the light. Then we saw hands reach out from the light. I didn't see her go, but my guides told me she was safe with her mother. A short while later the people who lived there did some research on the property that had stood on the ground before their house was built. They found an account that a young girl Lucy, aged eight, had been killed by her father after he had killed her mother. It said she was killed by a single blow to the head.

Another house had a terrible smell all the time. It was like rotting flesh. A friend from church and I went off to have a look. The house was new, but we had to agree there was a bad smell, even though it was masked by a lot of air fresheners. We traced the problem to the landing area. We linked into the energy to see what we could sense. As we stood with our eyes closed, I sensed someone was there. I opened one eye to have a look, and it was the family cat who had come to have a look at what we were doing. I am scared of cats, so I let out a yell that frightened my friend. The cat ran off, and we were left giggling at the situation. After we had composed ourselves, we found it was a problem of many layers. The first energy was fairly recent, just before the houses were built. We dealt with this and then found another level from about four hundred years ago. This was a time of great superstition, and the area was well known for the persecution of anyone found involved in witchcraft, even if they were innocent. We dealt with this layer and found yet another layer which went back about six hundred years. We both thought it had to do with a plague and a lot of people buried in a pit. The ground itself needed cleansing of the energy. After we had finished, we left a large clear crystal hanging on the landing to bring in some positive energy. When the lady came home, the first thing she noticed was that the smell had gone, so hopefully it all settled down after that.

I had a call from a young mother whose house was infested with huge flies. This was during the winter, and she said she could vacuum them up from the window on a night and the next morning more would be there. Also, her baby was unsettled, and she had sensed a presence in the house. She was so scared that she was staying with a relative and wouldn't go back to the house. As soon as I entered the house, I saw the spirit of an old lady lying at the bottom of the stairs. I asked the lady to try to get up, but she said she couldn't. She had been coming downstairs in her old slippers and had fallen down the stairs and banged her head. I helped her up and sat her on a chair. She asked me to tell her sister she had fallen over and hurt herself. I wondered if the flies were attracted to the energy, as the poor woman might have lain there for days or longer. So what to do? My guides said to ask someone from spirit to come for her, which I did. As I looked out of her kitchen window, I saw a young man in an army uniform. He was beckoning to her to come and join him. I pointed him out to her, and she said, "That's my George. That's my husband. It can't be. He was killed in the war." I encouraged her to go to him. As she ran into his arms, they both disappeared.

One stretch of road had a lot of accidents, so I took some members of my closed circle out there one night to see if we could find anything. It was dark, so no one could see us and wonder what we were up to. We all stood in a circle and linked hands. As we stood, each trying to see if we could sense anything, I noticed an extra hand on top of one of the ladies hands. Knowing it didn't belong to any of us, I took a photograph and was surprised to see when I later downloaded it that where the hand had been was a large orb.

While travelling on that bit of road myself, I was thinking about the church service I had just been to, when I saw a lady standing in the middle of the road right in my path. I put my foot on the brake and heard the loud tooting of a horn from the car behind. When I looked in the mirror, the man behind me, who had almost run into me, was shouting all sorts of abuse, and when I looked back at the road in front of me, there was no one there. Then I realised that the figure I had seen had no aura and thus must have been a spirit. A few years later I was driving down the same road when I saw her again. This time I closed my eyes and drove straight on, checking in the rear mirror that everything was all right. I smiled to myself, thinking that if I had hit a person, how I would explain that I ran into her because I thought it was a ghost!

Even more recently, again on the same road, I was in a bit of a rush to get to a committee meeting for church. I was suddenly aware of a change in energy. I can't explain it any better than that. Out of the corner of my eye I saw the spirit sort of half in the car and half on the road as if I had run into her. Of course, as quick as it happened, there was no one there. I slowed up and drove much slower the rest of the way and arrived late. When asked why I was late, I answered, "Because I ran over a bloody ghost!"

One day while I was treating a client, my dad from the spirit world appeared in front of me and told me that my auntie (my mother's sister) was with him. I said, "No, is Aunty Kitty dead?"

He smiled and said, "Well she is here with us. Tell your mom."

Glancing at the clock, I noted it was 4.30 p.m., and as soon as I could, I hurried over to Mom's house. Obviously she hadn't received any phone calls as she was not upset or anything. When I told her about Dad's message, she replied, "You're wrong about this. I am sure my niece would have let me know."

Later on around 8.00 p.m. she had a call to say that Aunt Kitty had passed to spirit at 4.30 p.m. that afternoon.

Modern technology is wonderful, and a friend of mine has software for her computer called "New Energy Vision" that can see and photograph energy. Called NEV for short, more can be seen about NEV on her website, which is listed at the end of this book. One day we took NEV to a house which was experiencing problems. This particular spirit was from the 1600s. She was very bad-tempered and was sure we were intruders in her house. Outside I saw a vision of what looked like a settlement. It had small earth and grass dwellings and a fire where several people sat around cooking and talking. The spirit of the bad-tempered lady was still shouting abuse at us inside the house where we stood. I told my friend to focus the camera on a place by the back wall which was fitted with modern appliances and new cupboards. I pointed to where the spirit was standing, and she took some pictures.

We could see the modern wall with our eyes, but through the camera all we could see was an old wall with wooden shelves holding a few pots. We showed the owner of the house, who went and fetched an old picture of what the wall had looked like when they moved in ten years earlier. The image NEV was picking up was from the past, as I could see it. Great stuff! I am so glad that modern technology can show what I see. I don't feel so odd now others can see how I see the world.

One day we took NEV to an old farmhouse in Somerset which was experiencing quite a few problems. They said they thought a lot of the unsettled feelings were in the large kitchen. Immediately I saw a huge mass of black negative energy by the back wall and asked my friend to put NEV on the area. Straight away we saw a large black energy on the computer screen that NEV was picking up, almost like what I saw with my eyes. After we had done our clearing and cleansing work, we took another image and saw rainbow bands of colours going upwards right through the house.

Another time we took NEV to some sacred standing stones to take pictures of the energy around the stones and the ground that they stood on. We had some great images of both. That day I met a man who was sitting on the grass enjoying the sunshine. He asked what we were doing, and I told him. He said he was talking to the spirit world via a metal rod he was holding. When I asked what it was, he said it was a cross between a wand and mobile phone, and did I want to join him? My friend and husband walked away to carry on the photography. I talked for ages with this man. We covered many subjects. I can't recall much of what we talked about, but I knew it was important. It was as if everything we talked about went into my memory, but I can't remember what it was. He gave me some stones that he said were a gift from Merlin. Soon I realised the others were ready to go, so I got up to make a move, and he said, "Do you send healing to the earth?" I said I did, and he said, "She's a big girl. She can take care of herself. Send her a lot of love. Love her, and send healing to the many peoples of the many countries on earth."

While I was still thinking about this, I said goodbye and started walking back to the others. He hadn't asked my name, and as I walked away I asked spirit, "Is this man for real? If so, give me a sign."

We were fifty yards apart by now, and as I thought it, he turned, waved, and said, "Bye, Lyn."

UFOs

Most people have an opinion on UFOs. It seems everyone is either a firm believer or makes fun of the very idea. I have seen several strange things in the skies that don't seem to have a rational explanation. David and I did a lot of investigating about the subject. Many books were appearing on the subject, and nearly every week people would be flocking to one place or another where UFOs were supposed to have been seen. Wiltshire seemed to attract a lot of interest for UFO spotters, especially Warminster. There was something called Operation Blue Book which collected all the reports of unexplained phenomena, and just recently a lot of that information has been made public.

The first time I ever saw anything strange in the skies was when I was about ten. We were playing in the street just before it was getting dark, and the sky was very clear. We saw what appeared to be a flash of lightning. As we looked towards where it had come from, we realised that it was like grids of light forming a large square in the sky. There were four lines on each side, and a lot of people were coming out from the houses to look at it. It was flashing as bright as lightning, but it was always visible. No one had any idea what it was, and after about ten minutes it disappeared altogether.

Another time in Devon I saw thirteen lights that formed an upside down V in the sky. They were white and stayed completely still. I had the camera with me, so I was able to take three shots before they split up and shot out of sight, leaving nothing to show they had ever been there. In those days it was a 35mm film camera. I couldn't wait to get the film developed. When I collected it, I ripped open the packet and was disappointed that there weren't any pictures of the lights. Checking the negatives, I was shocked to see that the three shots I had taken were not only blank but had pinhole-like holes in them. All the film before and after was fine. I showed the negatives to a photographer friend who was as stumped as I was as to what could have caused the holes.

I suppose the most memorable thing I ever saw was while walking in a Cotswolds High Street. It was about 7.00 p.m. and dark. There were a lot of people about, and I was with my sister-in-law, who was a Jehovah's Witness. We saw a light like a fluorescent tube in a vertical position coming down over us very slowly. It lit the whole area as if it was daytime. Everyone stopped and looked up. The heat coming from it was amazing, and we all covered our heads with our hands. It hovered for about twenty seconds, and then, moving into a horizontal position, it shot off at a great speed. We all watched as it came to a halt again in the distance and once again turned into a vertical position and started to descend once more. My sister-in-law was really afraid and kept asking what it was. I told her I had no idea, but maybe it was a UFO? Taking the dogs out for a wee late at night and in the early hours, I have often seen strange lights, but nothing like this encounter.

Another thing I have never been able to explain is that some nights when David was asleep, he used to have very strange dreams of working with people from other planets. When he woke up, he would paint or draw them. They had to be in black and silver. He said this was important. Some nights I would wake up and find him talking in a strange language. Once while he was asleep I asked, "What are you talking about?"

Still asleep, he replied, "It's a special piece of electronic equipment we are working on. You wouldn't understand."

More recently I went to Avebury with Jak. We climbed Silbury Hill. When we got to the top, we started talking to a couple who had been there all night. They said just before dawn they had noticed a small blue light hovering in the sky for about thirty seconds. "When it got light, that was there," they said, pointing to the field below. There was a huge crop circle. It was in the shape of a scorpion. I had never seen a crop circle except in pictures. It was pretty impressive, measuring about one hundred yards long and with such precise detail. There were people looking at it from the side, and others sitting inside the crop circle meditating. We went back a month later after the crop had been harvested, and the pattern was still there as strong as ever.

People often ask me if I believe in ETs or aliens. I don't like those words and prefer to call them star people. I can't believe we are the only life in the universe and beyond, so, yes, I do believe. As I have already said, from a very early age I have been able to see auras. Occasionally I have seen people with no aura. I had to work out for myself that non-aura people were probably spirits. When I saw people without an aura and other people saw them as well, it made me wonder why they didn't have an aura. I know the aura starts to fade away when death is close, but some of the people I have seen are very much alive and have carried on with what appears to be a normal life. Recently we have heard that star people are living alongside us, so maybe they don't have an aura as we do, and these are the people I have seen?

So What Happened to David?

I had heard nothing from David for nearly twenty years, but one day the phone rang at home.

"It's David."

Just hearing his voice made me shake with fear. He wanted to meet up as he was in the town. My first thoughts were "No, no, no, no!" but he sounded so "normal" I agreed. He said he was so unhappy and desperate to escape the dark side. He told me he had married another three times and had four children. He had done very well and was very wealthy, having bought a lot of property and started two businesses. I knew this was true, as I had seen pictures in magazines and newspapers of him with well-known people. He looked like he was living the high life, always having an expensive car and a pretty young woman in tow, but at what cost? Now he had grown tired of it all and wanted to go back to where we started and work for the light. However, did he think he could escape that easily?

He thought I could help him. My life had always been for the light. The dark side had tempted me many times, asking me why I struggled. Even in sleep I would have dreams of being able to have anything I wanted. I was never tempted and would always wake up with a rapid heartbeat and shaking. Now after all he had put us through, he wanted my help. My gut instinct was to tell him to get lost, but instead I told him that I ran development classes to help people find their spiritual pathway, and he could join one if he wanted to.

Again his true side came out. He laughed and asked what I could possibly teach him. He had it all. He had power and influence beyond anything I could imagine. After we parted that night, he went to see my mother in our home town where we had first met. She felt sorry for him and allowed him to stay for a short while as it was snowing outside. After a hot drink, he left. We found out later that he had been mugged and beaten up. They even stole his designer shoes.

The last I heard he was living in a hostel for the homeless. Then I heard he had died almost blind, crippled, and homeless. He was an alcoholic. Many years later, a medium brought me a message from my dad, and then she brought David through. Still angry with him, I refused to speak to him. The medium calmly told me he had been my greatest teacher. If he hadn't treated me the way he did and made me live life on the edge and find the real me, I couldn't possibly do the work I do now.

I thought about the message all weekend, and on the following Monday while I was hoovering, I decided that now was the time to sort it out. I opened up to spirit and said, "If you want to speak to me, I am willing to speak to you."

I saw many of my relatives from spirit, and finally David appeared. He said he was sorry and repeated the medium's message that he had been my greatest teacher. I swore at him for ten minutes and threw the hoover at him in temper. Eventually, after I had told him exactly how I felt, he repeated that all he had done was to help me find the real me, and so we made our peace. He faded away and went back to the spirit world. I have never seen or heard from him since.

Past Lives

I do believe we have all been here before, and occasionally I have had flashbacks or visions of those lives. They are certainly not memories from this life. Once I was meditating and found myself in a forest. I was female and looked about twenty and was very thin and felt weak and ill. I had on a very ragged rough type of long dress, and I had something around me like a shawl, but it looked more like an old sack. What was very noticeable was that my right foot was wrapped in dirty rags, and I could feel the pain as I put my foot to the floor. I "knew" the foot had been caught in an animal trap. I was uneducated and a bit simple. I made herbal remedies, and people only came to me when they needed help. Other times they would pelt me with rotten fruit. This life didn't last long, and I died at about twenty-seven.

I am also drawn to the year 1688. I read anything I can find about this time. There is little memory attached to it, but it does give me butterflies when I try to remember anything. Once I went to a town near to where I lived with Jak. He had found a second-hand shop which was housed in a very old building. He wanted me to see it. We found the shop up an old cobbled driveway. It looked hundreds of years old. We went upstairs in the shop, and I could see the lights downstairs through large cracks in the floor. Suddenly I was in a different time. I heard horses galloping and saw the horsemen carrying torches of fire. There was a lot of shouting, and I was hiding in the shop. I knew they had come to get me. Then I was back in the present time. I told Jak what had happened, and we left quickly. At the top of the driveway, I glanced back and "saw" a person hanging in the courtyard. I felt it was me.

My protection guide has told me that he and I had a life together in the twelfth century. Again, I can't remember anything about this life. Once when I was in Istanbul, this guide told me that we had been there together in the past life. I walked around, but nothing triggered a memory except that I had a feeling of anxiousness and wanting to go home.

I also have fond memories of a life in Atlantis. Another of my guides said he was an apprentice to a priest in Atlantis, and I was there as well. Sometimes I have visions of what I think must be Atlantis. It was a lovely life which placed a great deal of importance on crystal energy.

When I was sixteen, I went to see a film called *Witchfinder General*. It was about Mathew Hopkins, who was well known in history for persecuting people and trying to prove they were involved in witchcraft. Half way through the film I had a panic attack. I had to be taken home and was off work with stress for six weeks. I saw the film again forty years later and thought it was silly, but halfway through I again became uneasy and had to turn it off.

I went to a past-life regression with Jak once. The medium gave me a life in London. My whole family had died of smallpox. There was only my sister and myself left alive, and of course we also eventually died of the disease. He then said, "When you were born, you brought the memory of the disease to this life. Ask your parents if you had any problems with your skin."

When I asked Mom, she confirmed that I did. The doctors were at a loss how to treat it, and I couldn't have anything but warm water on my skin for the first three weeks of my life. On the other hand, the medium couldn't find any past lives for Jak. He had said many times that he came from the future and has always had amazing ideas, which he says he remembers from the future.

When I was visiting the pyramids once with Jak, we went inside one of them. It wasn't what I thought it would be like. I felt nothing—no energies—which was disappointing. That night I dreamt of being in Egypt in the past. In that life, I was well into the dark magic and woke up screaming. Maybe that's why I am so strict about teaching protection to my students. I know first-hand how powerful and alluring the dark side can be.

Sometimes I just have a feeling that I have been somewhere before, but a lot of people experience this, don't they?

So much has changed spiritually since we entered the new Age of Aquarius. Maybe we can discuss that in more detail another time.

I feel the gentle nudge from my guide. "It's time," he says. I look at the clock and quietly tell the people in the circle who are meditating, "It's time to come back into the room."

As they slowly start to come back to their bodies, I hope they will find as much comfort and love from their spiritual journey as I have.

Contacts

WAG: www.wellingtonactiongroup.co.uk
NEV: www.thechangist.co.uk
Wellington Witch: www.wellingtonwitch.co.uk

About the Author and the Book

Lyn, a natural seer of spirit and a healer from birth, helps people who come to her in Somerset to develop their own spiritual gifts. Drawing on her lifetime of experience as a gifted teacher, she devotes her time to this end. From early childhood, she has intuitively made herb medicine and healed animals. This is the story of her own life's journey